CHUJ (MAYAN) NARRATIVES

Chuj (Mayan) Narratives

Folklore, History, and Ethnography
from Northwestern Guatemala

Nicholas A. Hopkins

UNIVERSITY PRESS OF COLORADO

LOUISVILLE

© 2021 by University Press of Colorado

Published by University Press of Colorado
245 Century Circle, Suite 202
Louisville, Colorado 80027
Manufactured in the United States of America

The University Press of Colorado is a proud member
of the Association of University Presses.

The University Press of Colorado is a cooperative publishing enterprise supported,
in part, by Adams State University, Colorado State University, Fort Lewis College,
Metropolitan State University of Denver, Regis University, University of Colorado,
University of Northern Colorado, University of Wyoming, Utah State University,
and Western Colorado University.

∞ This paper meets the requirements of the ANSI/NISO Z39.48-1992
(Permanence of Paper)

ISBN: 978-1-64642-129-9 (paperback)
ISBN: 978-1-64642-130-5 (ebook)
DOI: https://doi.org/10.5876/9781646421305
Library of Congress Cataloging-in-Publication Data

CONTENTS

CHUJ (MAYAN) NARRATIVES

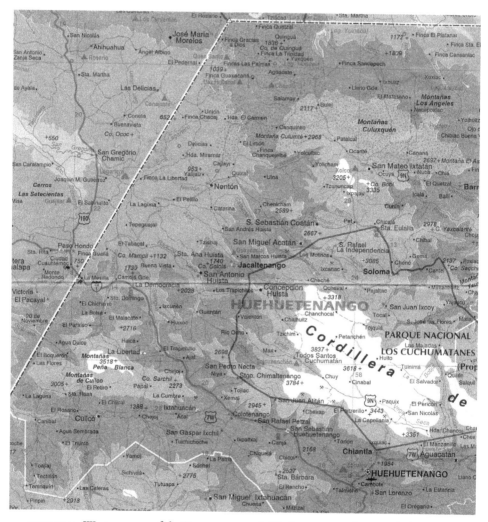

FIGURE 1.1. Western parts of the Departamento de Huehuetenango, Guatemala, bordering the Mexican state of Chiapas. After *Traveller's Reference Map of Guatemala and El Salvador.* International Map Productions, Vancouver, BC, Canada. ISBN 0-921463-64-2.

CHAPTER 1

Chuj Country

C HUJ IS A MAYAN LANGUAGE spoken in the northwest corner of the Department of Huehuetenango, Guatemala, and in adjacent areas across the international border in Mexico. There are two principal varieties of the language associated with the towns and municipios of San Mateo Ixtatán and San Sebastián Coatán. At the time represented by these stories, Chuj of both varieties extended into the neighboring municipio of Nentón, to the west. These narratives are all from the San Mateo variety of Chuj.

The areas occupied by the Chuj are dramatic. The town of San Mateo Ixtatán sits at an elevation of just under 8,400 feet above sea level (Dirección General de Cartografía 1962[2]:199). Surrounding peaks rise to 11,500 feet. Higher ground across the river valley from the town was covered by cloud forest until recent years. Down the river, called Titz'am in San Mateo ("mouth of the salt," salt mine) and Cambalam downstream to the east, the altitude falls sharply. At Barrillas, the next town, the altitude has dropped to about 4,600 feet above sea level (Dirección General de Cartografía 1962 [1]:37), a drop of some 3,800 feet. The moist gulf air that is pushed up the river valley shrouds San Mateo in a wet afternoon mist that drives people off the streets and into houses to sit next to the hearth.

Given the climate, it is no surprise that the name of the language derives from a prominent feature of households, the sweatbath. "Chuj" is a word that is ultimately of Mamean origin, but is used in local Spanish for the low structures that sit at the sides of houses, used for ordinary bathing as well as curing ceremonies. I once asked a man why they didn't bathe in the rivers, and he looked at me astonished and said, "Good Lord! Do you know how cold that water is?" It is likewise no surprise that the women's huipil (Chuj *nip*) is typically made of a double layer of heavy cotton cloth, with designs in thick embroidery covering the back and chest, and the traditional men's jacket, the *capixay*, is heavy wool. The latter is made by the men, who spin and weave the wool and put the garment together, adding a stitched design resembling a pectoral cross around

FIGURE 1.2. A typical sweatbath (Chuj *ikaj*). The Mam term
for sweatbath, *chuj*, provides the name of the language of their
northern neighbors. Patalcal, May 1965. Photo by author.

the neck. This element of clothing (Chuj *lopil*) must have been introduced by
priests from northwest Spain, because the Spanish word *capixay* comes from the
Basque *capo sayo*, vulture cape. These wool tunics are prominent in trade. Their
makers carry them across the Mexican border to Comitán, Chiapas, for sale;
throughout highland Chiapas they are known as *koton chuj* or just *chuj*, and
they are the typical men's jacket in Amatenango, between Comitán and San
Cristóbal de Las Casas.

A few miles west of San Mateo, the Ixtenam River (Chuj *yich tenam*, "at the
foot of the rock outcrop"), rises and flows west to meet the Grijalva River in
Chiapas, falling to about 2,000 feet above sea level near the Mexican border
in the municipio of Nentón (Dirección General de Cartografía 1962[1]:481).
Chuj country is thus typically high altitude valleys surrounded by higher peaks,
drained by swift-flowing streams. Access to water becomes a problem toward
the end of the dry season (December to May), when people may be forced to
walk miles to the nearest productive spring or waterhole. The desiccated vegetation in this period gives rise to brush fires that march unimpeded across the
landscape. Vegetation varies widely from low oak forests to high rain forests,
with cloud forests at higher elevations (see Breedlove and Hopkins 1970–71
for details).

FIGURE 1.3. The older design of the San Mateo Ixtatán huipil, *lak'an nip*. Photo by Elizabeth Purdum.

FIGURE 1.4. The newer design of the San Mateo Ixtatán huipil, *kolob' nip*. Photo by Elizabeth Purdum.

FIGURE 1.5. The San Mateo Ixtatán men's jacket, *lopil* (Spanish *capixay*). Photo by Elizabeth Purdum.

FIGURE 1.6. Vegetation along the trail from San Mateo Ixtatán to Bulej, May 1965. Photo by author.

In the 1960s, when these stories were collected, the official estimate of the number of Chuj speakers at the last census (and it was only a rough estimate) was 10,771 (Dirección General de Estadística 1950, Cuadro 29). The total population of the three municipios (San Mateo Ixtatán, San Sebastián Coatán, and Nentón) was 17,496. By 1964, a later census reported that total population figures had jumped to 28,214, an increase of more than 61 percent. The number of indigenous language speakers must have increased accordingly. If so, the number of Chuj speakers may have been around 17,000 in 1964.

At the time I did my field work there were virtually no published reports on the language. The missionary David Ekstrom (1961) had produced a partial San Mateo Chuj translation of the New Testament. Similar translations into San Sebastián Chuj had been made by Kenneth Williams (1963a, b, c), as well as a short grammatical sketch (Williams and Williams 1966). A few brief vocabulary lists had appeared in a variety of sources (Recinos 1954, Swadesh 1961, Mayers 1966), and Andrade (1946) had supplied some textual data. But there was no adequate description of the language to be consulted. As a result, I was assigned the task of producing the basic descriptive package of structural linguistics: a phonology, a grammar, and a set of texts.

My mentor and major professor, Norman A. McQuown, who had done his dissertation on Totonac under Edward Sapir, had inherited Manuel J. Andrade's Mayan materials when he came to teach at the University of Chicago, and he decided to direct research into the relatively undocumented family of Mayan languages. He set about assigning graduate students to one language after another, choosing the tasks according to the place of the language in the family, field conditions, and the abilities and weaknesses of the student. A major effort went into the Chiapas Study Projects, starting in the late 1950s and coordinated with Stanford and Harvard Universities, focused on the Chiapas Highlands. Harvard continued its concentrated research in Zinacantán (Vogt 1994); Stanford and Chicago took on the rest of the Tzotzil and Tzeltal communities (McQuown and Pitt-Rivers 1970). My first field experience, 1960–62, was with this project. Married couples with children were given assignments that kept them in more civilized conditions. As an expendable bachelor, I was assigned to the north Tzotzil area and specifically to San Pablo Chalchihuitán, where the Cuban anthropologist Calixta Guiteras Holmes had done basic ethnographic work (Guiteras Holmes 1951).

San Pablo Chalchihuitán was a small community with a ceremonial center located on a ledge beneath a mountain massif that had kept its population—located on the other side of the ridge—free of contact with the outside world since the Conquest. There was only one non-Indian (Ladino) resident in the village,

FIGURE 1.7. *Capitanes* perform at the crosses in front of the church in the center of downtown San Pablo Chalchihuitán, Chiapas, 1961. Photo by the author.

doubling as the schoolteacher and *secretario municipal*. No electricity, no plumbing, no stores, and no road connecting it to the outside. It was good preparation for San Mateo Ixtatán. In 1964, when I told John Avant, a friend who had done ethnographic survey work in Guatemala, that for my dissertation work I had been assigned to San Mateo Chuj, he just laughed and said, "If you liked Chalchihuitán, you'll love San Mateo!" The first passable road connecting San Mateo to the departmental capital at Huehuetenango had been blazed just a year or so before by the army, under the threat to local Indian authorities of cutting out their tongues if they objected, and the road still had sections of "corduroy," logs laid across the road for traction on muddy slopes.

Fortunately, among the many things McQuown taught his students was that you didn't have to suffer more than necessary. Getting the work done was the main thing. While ethnographers and social anthropologists have to be present in their field areas as "participant observers," taking part in community affairs and constantly observing the goings-on, linguists have the luxury of being able to remove themselves to a more comfortable setting, away from the complications and constant interruptions of village life. What we need to know resides largely in the mind of any one speaker of the language, so acquire a good speaker to help you and go somewhere you can concentrate on the research without having to maintain community relations (and where you have electricity, hot showers, and cold beer).

FIGURE 1.8. San Mateo Ixtatán (*ko chonhab'*, "our town"), seen across the valley from the road to Barillas. August 1964. Photo by author. The road from Huehuetenango is visible above the town. Below it, the church, and to the left the school and the precolumbian ruins of Guaxaclajún (*Wajxaklajunh*, "eighteen").The salt mines lie below the town, above the (unseen) river.

My first excursion to San Mateo was with the goal of finding a good language consultant. The Catholic priest, Father Arthur Nichols, recommended a man who had served him as simultaneous translator, Francisco Santizo Andrés. We talked and he agreed to come to Huehuetenango for a trial two weeks, after which we would decide if we wanted to work together. We both enjoyed the experience so much that we continued to work together for a little more than a year. During that time I accumulated some four hours of recorded tape (160 pages of transcription) from Francisco, and on excursions into the field another six hours (525 pages) from other speakers, as well as two dozen dialect survey questionnaires that covered the area of San Mateo Chuj speech. We also collected and identified hundreds of plants (Breedlove and Hopkins 1970–71) and recorded ethnographic information about topics like kinship, salt production, the Mayan calendar, geographical place names, and, of course, a corpus of folktales and narratives. Some of this material has been published, some awaits discussion. All the recorded material has been archived at AILLA (www.ailla.utexas.org, the Archive of the Indigenous Languages of Latin America), including the recorded performances of the narratives presented here.

The situation of Chuj and the speakers of Chuj has changed drastically since my field work was carried out. The devastation of the Guatemalan civil war ("*la violencia*") hit the Chuj area hard. Dozens of villages were destroyed or abandoned. Population fled to Mexico and on to the United States, where there are Chuj colonies in California, Virginia, North Carolina, and Florida (at least). New populations flowed in to fill the empty spaces, so the current demography is nothing like it was when my study was done. The Summer Institute of Linguistics (Ethnologue.com) estimates there are 41,600 Chuj speakers in Guatemala, and another 1,770 elsewhere (but this refers only to Tziscao, Chiapas, and other populations in Mexico, and not the populations in the United States).

The status of linguistic studies has also changed drastically. The Proyecto Lingüístico Francisco Marroquín (PLFM), initiated by Maryknoll priests but picked up by North American linguists when the former were expelled from the country, has trained several generations of native Mayan language speakers, including Chuj, and turned the direction of the Proyecto over to its graduates. That organization has in turn spawned the Academia de las Lenguas Mayas de Guatemala (ALMG) and other activist groups, and these have negotiated educational and cultural reforms with the Guatemalan government, including a set of official orthographies that have replaced the ad hoc creations of missionaries and dilettantes (Lenguas Mayas de Guatemala 1988). A very active publication program operates under the rubrics of PLFM and Cholsamaj, among others. This movement has produced two Chuj-Spanish dictionaries (Felipe Diego and Gaspar Juan 1998, Academia de Lenguas Mayas de Guatemala 2003), with other material available on the internet. An American linguist working with PLFM, Judith Maxwell, now at Tulane University, was a consultant on the dictionary project, and has produced a dissertation on Chuj (Maxwell 1978b) as well as a number of scholarly articles (Maxwell 1976–2001). My own dictionary of Chuj is an on-line publication (Hopkins 2012a). A Mexican linguist, Cristina Buenrostro, at the Instituto de Investigaciones Antropológicas, Universidad Nacional Autónoma de México, has worked with the Mexican Chuj colony at Tziscao and produced a series of works (Buenrostro 2002–13). A recent addition to the repertory are the works of Jessica Coon at McGill University (Coon 2016, Coon and Carolan 2017).

The academic reader will note that there is no attention given here to linguistic theory nor is there reference to literary analysis, beyond noting some aspects of the discourse strategies of the narrators. This is deliberate. My purpose is descriptive and empirical, to present to those who would wish to see such analyses the material they would need to do the job, and to introduce the language and its oral literature to students and others.

A Note on Language Relations and Prehistory

The Mayan language most closely related to Chuj is Tojolabal (sssat.missouri. edu), whose speakers reside to the west in adjacent parts of the eastern extremes of the state of Chiapas, Mexico, between the border and the town of Comitán. The subgroup of Mayan composed of Chuj and Tojolabal is called Chujean (chart 1). Mexican Tojolabals make an annual pilgrimage to San Mateo to carry out rituals and take home salt, and it is reasonable to postulate that the ancestors of the Tojolabal came from the Cuchumatanes area and expanded into lowland Chiapas. According to the approximate dating of glottochronology, the native and migrant populations would have achieved effective separation by about 1,600 years ago, or somewhere around 400 AD (in terms of Mayan archaeology, in the Early Classic; language classifications and all glottochronological figures are from Kaufman 1978:959; for a detailed discussion of the family, see Campbell 2017).

CHART 1. The Mayan Languages

Huastecan
Huastec (Wastek, Teenek), Chicomuseltec (Chikomuseltek, Kabil)

Yucatecan
Yucatec Maya (Maya, Yucatec), Lacandón (Lakantun); Itzaj (Itzá), Mopan (Mopán)

Western Mayan
Cholan: Ch'ol (Chol), Chontal (Yokot'an); Ch'orti' (Chortí) and extinct
   Ch'olti' (Choltí)
Tzeltalan: Tseltal (Tzeltal), Tsotsil (Tzotzil)
Kanjobalan: Q'anjob'al (Kanjobal), Akatek (Acatec), Popti' (Jacaltec); Mocho'
   (Mochó, Tuzantek, Motozintlec)
Chujean: Chuj, Tojol-abal (Tojolabal)

Eastern Mayan
Quichean: Q'eqchi' (Kekchí), Uspantek (Uspantec); Poqom (Poqomam, Poqomchi');
   K'iche' (Quiché), Kaqchikel (Cakchiquel), Tz'utujil, Sakapultek (Sacapultec),
   Sipakapense (Sipacapeño)
Mamean: Mam, Tektitek (Teco), Awakatek (Aguacatec), Ixil (Ixhil)

Language names not in parentheses are the preferred current usage (Aissen et al. 2017:8–9), names in parentheses are traditional and alternative names. Many more variants exist, and preferences are in constant flux. Family subdivision names are those established in modern literature; all but Huastecan constitute Southern Mayan. Western and Eastern Mayan together constitute Central Mayan (Kaufman 2017:66–67).

Surrounding Chuj on the south and east are varieties of the Kanjobalan (Q'anjob'alan) languages: from west to east Jacaltec, Acatec, and Kanjobal proper (Popti', Akateko, and Q'anjob'al). This subgroup is the closest relative of Chujean, sharing a common ancestor that existed around 100 BC (in the very Late Preclassic). Chujean and Kanjobalan constitute "Greater Kanjobalan," The situation of these languages within the Western branch of Mayan suggests that their ancestors in turn became distinct from their nearest relatives after migrating into the Cuchumatanes from the riverine areas to the east, the lower Ixcán and Chixoy Rivers, by about 1,000 BC (in the Middle Preclassic). Shortly thereafter a similar movement into the Chiapas Highlands resulted in the diversification of the remaining riverine group, "Greater Cholan," evolving into Tzotzilan (Tzeltal and Tzotzil) in the Chiapas highlands and leaving Cholan (which later became Chontal [Yokot'an], Chol [Ch'ol], and Chortí [Ch'orti']) in the riverine lowlands.

The two large subgroups of languages Greater Kanjobalan and Greater Cholan constitute the branch of the Mayan family known as Western Mayan, in contrast to Eastern Mayan, the languages of the Guatemalan highlands. The Mayan family consists of these languages (which form Central Mayan) plus Yucatecan (to form Southern Mayan) and Huastecan (Kaufman 2017). The diversification of the family was effective by about 2,100 BC (that is, by the Early Preclassic), and probably involved dispersion from a common homeland into the Yucatán Peninsula and the upper Gulf Coast (Yucatecan and Huastecan, respectively), into the lowland riverine and piedmont areas of Guatemala (Western Mayan), and into the Guatemalan Highlands (Eastern Mayan).

Differences within the Cuchumatán languages (Greater Kanjobalan) came about at least in part by differential influences from their neighbors to the north and south. A chart of shared innovations (Josserand 1975:503, fig. A) shows that Tojolabal and Chuj (as well as Tzotzilan) share several phonological innovations with Cholan and Yucatecan Mayan to the north, the languages most involved in Classic Mayan culture. Kanjobalan languages share one of these innovations, but also share innovations with Eastern Mayan languages to the south. The Cuchumatanes is thus a "shatter zone," an area of closely related languages that is splintered by differential external influences. In fact, the most notable difference between the two varieties of Chuj, the loss of vowels and the reduction of resultant consonant clusters in San Sebastián Coatán Chuj, resembles features of the development of the Mamean languages that extend northward into the Cuchumatanes. In grammar and lexicon, the creation of the noun classifiers that characterize Chujean and Kanjobalan languages (and some varieties of Mam) has been attributed to the influence of Chiapanec, a dominant Otomanguean neighbor to the west, in late pre-Columbian times (Hopkins 2012b).

Early and insightful ethnographic work was done in the Cuchumatanes by Maud Oakes on Mam-speaking Todos Santos Cuchumatán (1951), by Oliver LaFarge on a Kanjobal community, Santa Eulalia (1947), and by LaFarge and Douglas Byers on Jacaltenango (1931). Frans Blom and LaFarge made archaeo-logical, ethnographic, and linguistic notes as they traveled through the area in 1926–27. The status of ethnographic knowledge at mid-twentieth century was briefly summarized by Charles Wagley (1969). A similar report on mid-century linguistic work was compiled by William Bright (1967), and McQuown (1967) sketched earlier work on Mesoamerican languages sources, beginning with Eu-ropean contact. Hopkins and Josserand (1994) have outlined trends in Mayan linguistics from the Colonial period to the present.

Field Work in the Chuj Region

The narratives presented here were gathered during my dissertation field work in 1964–65. My first exposure to the Chuj language was in 1962, when I went to the Department of Huehuetenango, Guatemala, with Norman A. McQuown and Brent Berlin to gather data on the languages of the Cuchumatanes (Berlin et al. 1969). At the time I was a graduate student in the Linguistics Program at the University of Texas at Austin. Like Berlin, I was temporarily employed as a research assistant on the University of Chicago's Chiapas Study Projects, directed by McQuown (McQuown and Pitt-Rivers 1970; Hopkins 1964b, 1967a,b, 1969, 1970a, 1974). Working through the Maryknoll priests who were then the Catholic clergy in the indigenous areas of Huehuetenango and else-where in Guatemala, we recorded material, usually in the form of 100-word Swadesh lists (for glottochronology), from several languages. The sample in-cluded two speakers of San Mateo Ixtatán Chuj, including the man who was later to become my tutor.

In the spring of 1962, as field work for the Chiapas project wound down, I returned to Austin to finish drafting my master's thesis (Hopkins 1964a), and then went on to Chicago to begin graduate studies in anthropology at the Uni-versity of Chicago, with McQuown as my major professor. I continued to work on Chiapas project materials in McQuown's archives, and in 1963 he assigned me the Chuj language as the topic of my upcoming doctoral dissertation (Hop-kins 1967a). Over the next academic year I transcribed and analyzed the Chuj

FIGURE 1.9. Huehuetenango. The yellow house on the corner (with a door and two windows) was my home and project headquarters, shared with Francisco Santizo Andrés. In the background, the Cuchumatán Mountains. Photo by the author.

materials we had collected and prepared preliminary analyses of the phonology and morphology of the language. During this period I also worked as a laboratory assistant in the Language Lab at the University of Chicago, and I am indebted to its technical director, Don Ledine, for teaching me the proper protocols for recording, handling, and preserving magnetic tape recordings.

At the end of the summer of 1964, with support from a National Defense Education Act Foreign Language Fellowship, I went to Huehuetenango to begin field work on Chuj. By the end of August I had contracted a native speaker of Chuj, Francisco Santizo Andrés, and rented a house in the city of Huehuetenango, where we began work in earnest. From then until September of 1965 we worked an eight-hour day, six days a week, with occasional breaks when Francisco would go home and I would go to San Cristóbal de Las Casas, where Berlin and other anthropologists and linguists were working on their own projects.

We began by reviewing my preliminary analyses and correcting my errors of transcription, as well as my phonemic analysis. Francisco had worked as a simultaneous translator for the San Mateo Maryknoll priest, Father Arthur Nichols, and he had a keen sense of language. He quickly pointed out errors in my analysis, including the missed contrast between the consonants written here as /j/

and /h/, velar and laryngeal fricatives. Chuj is one of the few Mayan languages to preserve this contrast from Proto-Mayan (see Kaufman 2003). I learned later that Kenneth Williams, the Protestant missionary working on San Sebastián Coatán Chuj, had caught the contrast, but his Summer Institute of Linguistics colleagues refused to accept his analysis, to his great frustration. Based on the revised analysis of the phonology, Francisco and I agreed on a technical orthography for Chuj, using the cent sign for /tz/ ([ts]), the letters <c> and <s> with hachek for /ch/ and /x/ ([tʃ] and [ʃ]), the letter <x> for /j/, and so forth. This was reasonable at the time, since we were decades away from the era of practical orthographies.

Francisco mastered the new way of writing without delay, and we began to record short narratives dictated by him: an encounter in the market with a friend from home, a short biographical sketch, accounts of agriculture and salt production; see the archives at AILLA (the Archive of the Indigenous Languages of Latin America, www.ailla.utexas.org) for these recordings. Francisco would dictate a text to the tape recorder, operated by me, and then transcribe the tape, preparing a Spanish glossing if necessary (see Hopkins 1980b, a text on salt production). I would go over the transcriptions and ask questions about the grammar and lexicon. All the lexical material gathered by these techniques was put on three-by-five-inch slips and filed in the lexical file that is the basis for my dictionary of Chuj (Hopkins 2012a). I also used a technique devised by Terry Kaufman for Mayan languages, the Monosyllable Dictionary, to elicit vocabulary. This technique involves constructing all the possible CVC sequences (Consonant-Vowel-Consonant, the most common root shape in Mayan) and trying to find lexical items based on each. Surprising things emerge that neither speaker nor linguist would expect.

After a field trip to the San Mateo area in February 1965, to collect plants with Dennis Breedlove (Breedlove and Hopkins 1970–71), in May of 1965 Francisco and I carried out a two-week dialect survey of the area in which San Mateo Ixtatán Chuj was spoken, in the municipios of San Mateo Ixtatán and Nentón, collecting material from seventeen aldeas and the town center, a total of twenty-seven questionnaires. (No regional patterns of distinction were noted.) Several texts were recorded during this field season and as usual the transcribed material was incorporated into my lexical files. Back in Huehuetenango, Francisco spent his time transcribing the material we had collected and consulting with me as questions arose. When a topic came up, we would extend the lexical data by eliciting more items in the same domain, that is, animal names (Hopkins 1980a), place names (Hopkins 1972), and other lexical and ethnographic

FIGURE 1.10. Cloud forest vegetation featuring tree ferns. The first time my botanist colleague Dennis Breedlove saw these, he thought they were palm trees—until he saw the spore spots on the undersides of the fronds! Photo by the author.

material. Since that was the era of ethnoscience, some research was done into the semantic structures of these domains (Hopkins 2006). When the transcription of a narrative was finished, I would prepare an English translation on the basis of the Chuj original with support from Francisco's rough Spanish glossing. We also worked on numeral classifiers, and I was engaged with Brent Berlin and Chris Day in a comparative study of this domain in Chuj, Tzeltal, and Jacaltec Maya (Hopkins 1970b).

I returned to Chicago in September 1965, to finish my graduate work and my doctoral dissertation. I then took a job teaching anthropology at the University of Texas in Austin, and continued to process my Chuj materials. I married Kathryn Josserand in 1970 and spent a year in Milwaukee, where she had been teaching, and then returned to Texas. In 1973 we left Texas for Mexico City at the invitation of Angel Palerm to establish the Programa de Lingüística at the new Centro de Investigaciones Superiores del INAH that he directed (CISINAH, now CIESAS, the Centro de Investigaciones y Estudios Superiores en Antropología Social). Work on Chuj was abandoned in favor of field training and research on languages closer to Mexico City, especially Otomanguean languages (Hopkins and Josserand 1979). A few years later, because we had begun to follow the developments in Maya epigraphy, we began to work on Mayan languages

FIGURE I.II. The San Mateo aldea Patalcal (*pat alkal*, "house of the mayor"), May 1965. The entire countryside was shrouded with smoke from an uncontrolled brush fire. Photo by the author.

FIGURE I.I2. A typical house in Patalcal: walls of adobe, roof of wood shingles. The porch and patio in front of the house are the principal work areas. Photo by the author.

again, but field work was on Chol, not Chuj (Hopkins and Josserand 2016). We returned to the United States in 1982 and spent some ten years hustling a living with grant support, workshops on Maya hieroglyphic writing, and leading tours to the Maya areas we knew from field work. In 1991 Kathryn took an academic

FIGURE 1.13. During our dialect survey, tin roofing arrives for the new Catholic church in the aldea of Xubojasun (*xub'oj asun*, "breath of the clouds"), municipio of Nentón. May 1965. Photo by the author.

FIGURE 1.14. Cross shrine on a rock outcrop on the outskirts of the aldea of Canquintic (*k'ankintik*, meaning unknown), municipio of Nentón. May 1965. A woman in a red huipil kneels to the left of the cross. Entering the village with a loaded mule, I was hailed by a woman who ran from her house to ask "*Tas ha chonho'?*," What are you selling? Photo by the author.

job at Florida State University and I began to work there as an adjunct professor. We concentrated our field work on Chol and our academic work on Maya hieroglyphics.

I did not return to work on Chuj until 2005–6, when I received a National Endowment for the Humanities Documenting Endangered Languages Fellowship.

FIGURE 1.15. On the trail in the Yolcultac (*yol k'ultak*, "center of the brushland") forest, municipio of Nentón. May 1965, at the end of the dry season. Photo by the author.

This fellowship allowed me to prepare my Chuj materials for digitization and archiving at AILLA. All my recorded materials on Chuj are archived there, along with my transcribed Field Notes and Field Photos, and a revised version of my dissertation (in a modern orthography). The collection includes some forty samples of Chuj speech from eight Chuj settlements, some of which no longer exist. More than twenty of the settlements reported in my inventory of place names were abandoned or destroyed in the genocide of the so-called civil war (Manz 1988:83–89).

In the summer of 2011, I dug out of a closet a wooden chest that contained four drawers of lexical slip files, untouched since about 1970. Over the next few months I transcribed the lexical entries into an electronic text file, using the practical orthography that I had designed for Chuj; the now-official orthographies did not exist at the time (Lenguas Mayas de Guatemala 1988). These transcriptions included all the data on plant and animal names, place names, numeral classifiers, and so forth, that I had previously published. The resulting dictionary (Hopkins 2012a), which includes a grammar sketch, is housed on the website of the Foundation for the Advancement of Mesoamerican Studies, Inc. (www.famsi.org/mayawriting/dictionary/Hopkins/dictionaryChuj.html), now administered by the Los Angeles County Museum of Art. I continue to unearth and revise Chuj materials (Hopkins 2012b), and after publishing on Chol folktales (Hopkins and Josserand 2016) I turned back to the Chuj texts I had collected some fifty years earlier. A sample of those texts constitutes the present collection.

A Note on Orthography

In my field work with Francisco Santizo Andrés, we used a technical linguistic orthography that used the cent sign <¢> and a letter <c> with hachek (as in Czech orthography) for the affricates, an <x> for the velar fricative, and other conventions of contemporary linguistic usage. When I prepared my material for archiving at AILLA, I transcribed my Chuj material into a practical orthography of my own design. Now, a set of new orthographies for Mayan languages has been negotiated between Maya activists from the Academia de las Lenguas Mayas de Guatemala, the Proyecto Lingüístico Francisco Marroquín and other native-speaker organizations. The Chuj narratives that follow have been retranscribed to follow the norms of *Lenguas Mayas de Guatemala* (1988). Note that despite efforts to standardize, there is still considerable variation in the orthographies used by Mayanist scholars (Aissen et al. 2017:9–11).

Elsewhere my Chuj materials have been presented in my earlier orthography. For those who wish to consult that material, the changes from the official orthography are the following: I write glottal stop as <7>, following Kaufman (2003), and I write it thus in all positions. The official orthography does not write word-initial glottal stops, which are implied by a word-initial vowel, and writes them elsewhere as <'>, the same as the glottalization on consonants. The alveolar affricates are written <tz, tz'> instead of <ts, ts'>. The glottalized bilabial stop is written <p'> instead of <b'>. I do write the velar nasal <nh>, as it is written here (in my dissertation it was written <N>, and <ng> would be a reasonable option). All these choices have linguistic motivations, but orthographies are not strictly linguistic devices, and I support Maya activists in their preferences.

CHAPTER 2

Narratives in Chuj

T HIS COLLECTION OF SIX narratives told in Chuj demonstrates the broad variety of stories people tell one another and the variety of sources of those stories: personal narratives, legendary events, mythological tales, and stories borrowed from other cultures. All were recorded by me during field work on Chuj from 1964 to 1965. (See the Archive of the Indigenous Languages of Latin America, www.ailla.utexas.org, for these and other samples of Chuj speech recorded during field work; AILLA reference codes for each text are given below and at the head of each transcription.)

Introduction to the Texts

Two of the stories are ultimately of foreign origin, but their origins are not the same. In one case, the story known to the narrator as An Old Man Whose Son Killed Him [CAC 002 R022], the story clearly comes from the European tradition, and must have been introduced to the Chuj by schoolteachers. It is the classic Greek tale of a couple whose child is destined to kill his father and how that came about, including the solution to a famous riddle: What animal walks on four legs at dawn, on two legs at noon, and on three legs in the evening?

The other tale, Coyote and Rabbit [CAC 002 R027], is probably ultimately of African origin, although some of its episodes are traditional in the American South and may have been introduced secondhand to the Chuj. This is the series of incidents that make up the Br'er Rabbit stories, stories that reflected earlier African tales involving Hyena instead of Fox (Diarassouba 2007). Here the story features Coyote instead of either Fox or Hyena. Coyote stories and stories of Rabbit Trickster abound in the native New World, and some of the episodes may be of American origin, adapted to the framework of the African stories. Some episodes have a local flavor (such as misty mountains) and are likely of local origin.

A third story, Friend of the Animals [CAC 002 R020], expresses such a universal theme that it could possibly be of foreign origin as well, but it has elements that suggest it is native. First, the moral of the story, that good acts are reciprocated, is basic to Maya belief (but not, of course, unique to that culture). Second, some of the incidents are similar to events related in the Popol Vuh, a sixteenth-century collection of Highland Guatemalan mythology, legend, and history (Christenson 2007). Finally, the relationship between the two protagonists, a good younger brother and an evil elder brother, is also present in known Mayan tales (see Hopkins and Josserand 2016:41–58), but of course it is likewise not unique to the Maya. Arguing for a native origin is the fact that the story contains no foreign elements. Critical events in An Old Man Whose Son Killed Him feature a card game and a pistol, and then there is that riddle. Coyote and Rabbit is filled with foreign elements: a tar baby and a cheese, for instance. But Friend of the Animals has no such non-Maya features.

The fourth story, The Sorcerer [CAC 002 R012], is clearly of native origin, because it relates events said to have occurred in the Chuj communities within living memory. It is local history even though it treats supernatural phenomena that an outsider might consider inventions of a creative mind. But these are the parameters of local understanding of events. Not all that happens is easily explained in terms of Western empirical science; other forces may well be behind the events, and in fact are assumed to be present in local worldview. That people have companion animals, and powerful people have correspondingly powerful animals, is taken for granted, and it explains a lot of things that have hidden causes. (For other manifestations of this belief system, see Guiteras Holmes 1961 for Tzotzil and Pitarch 1996 for Tzeltal.)

The story about The Communists [CAC 002 R036] is again local history. The evil elements present are not supernatural nor are they easily controlled. This story anticipates the terrible events that were to ravage the Chuj area some decades later and result in the diaspora of the Chuj people. It concerns the early stages of what is called *la violencia*, the government's war on its most vulnerable populations, a civil war whose consequences are still felt.

The final narration, Taking Out the Salt [CAC 002 R008], is an extended monologue that outlines the production of San Mateo's famous black salt. To an extraordinary degree the salt trade pervades San Mateo society—economics, politics, and religion are all involved and both genders and all social levels participate.

The presentation of these narratives is in matched columns of Chuj and English, and these stories appear here for the first time in English translation. Insofar as possible, the translation matches the Chuj line for line, but of course this is not always possible. However, the sense of the Chuj is preserved to the extent that a translation to a foreign language can do so. The Chuj text was transcribed directly from the tape recordings made in the field, and the transcriptions were done by a speaker of the same variety of the language. They were checked by me against the tapes, and I translated the tales directly to English. For those who wish to delve deeper into the original language of the narrations, I have appended a grammar sketch, summarized my thesis [CAC 002 R065], and employed the official Chuj orthography. An independently derived grammar of Chuj by the Mexican linguist Cristina Buenrostro is also posted in the AILLA archive [CAC 004 R001]. See also my Chuj-English dictionary [CAC 002 R066].

I have tried to avoid excessive editing. Mistakes and hesitations have been left in the text, although some of them are marked by parentheses or brackets. Preliminary conversations and closing statements are intact, and the transcriptions generally represent everything that is on the tape. That is, I want these stories to be presented as they were told; I do not want to try to outguess the speakers and change the language they employed, even if it might in some way "improve" the text.

In my opinion, the presentation of native oral literature is all too often edited to "improve" it. The worst-case scenario is when the texts are not presented in the original language at all, but are retold in a different language and in a style more familiar to the Western reader. The rough content of the story is preserved, but not the style of its telling. This is a common tendency in collections that are destined to be used in schools; out of a mistaken conception of respect for the native tradition, the translators want the stories to fit into a familiar—and more prestigious—canon. My favorite commentary on this sort of presentation is that of the Australian aborigine scholar, T. G. H. Strehlow (1947), in his introduction to the complex and beautiful tales of the Aranda. In order to illustrate how aboriginal oral literature was normally presented (in pidgin English translation), Strehlow gives parallel treatment to the Shakespearian play *Macbeth*, a jewel of English literature. The result (reproduced in Hymes 1964:80) is both hilarious and sobering: [ole lady Muckbet:] "Me properly sorry longa that ole man, me bin finishem; him bin havem too much blood, poor beggar. . . .").

Even when the text is presented in the native language, "needless" repetitions may be eliminated, when repetition is one of the most characteristic devices in Maya literature, without which the tale can hardly be called Maya. And as we discovered working with Chol storytellers (Hopkins and Josserand 2016), the introductory remarks that are often edited out as "not part of the story" ("This is a story I learned when . . .") are in fact an expected element in storytelling. You might as well delete from Lincoln's Gettysburg Address the opening sentence

("Four score and seven years ago . . ."), since it is just background information, "not part of the story" (which might be said to begin with "Now we are engaged in a great civil war . . ."). Since before learning better I was guilty of the same, I am particularly sensitive about this.

I do regret not recording more stories. At the time there were two reasons for this. Since my primary goal was to write a sketch of the phonology and morphology of the language, I really only collected texts in order to have extended samples of language that I could scan for instances of grammar and lexicon (the former destined for Hopkins 1967a, the latter compiled as Hopkins 2012a). The expected "package" for a linguistics dissertation in those days was the phonology, the morphology, and sample texts; syntax was not yet the principal (even the sole) focus of a thesis as it is today. The second reason I didn't record more texts in the field was that the recording device was a battery-powered Uher tape recorder, and recording ate up batteries at a frightful rate. Since there was no electrical power and no source for batteries anywhere outside major towns, all the batteries for a two-week field trip had to be carried in. I didn't even record most of my field interviews for this reason; while my Chuj was not fluent, I could at least do running transcriptions of wordlists during the interviews.

I believe that none of us anticipated the rate at which things could change among the indigenous populations we work with. There was a tendency to think of these societies as unchanging over time, although nothing could be further from the truth. I once believed that the women's huipils and men's clothing that I saw in highland Chiapas were so traditional that they must have been the same for decades if not centuries. Then I became aware of old photographs of people from the region, and it was obvious that features that I took to be fixed diagnostics for certain villages were in fact changing all the time. When I was working in San Mateo Ixtatán, the woolen tunic *capixays* worn by the men had vestigial sleeves, about elbow length but too narrow to accommodate the arm; they stuck out over the upper arms. I was told that a couple of generations earlier the sleeves had been wrist length, and men actually put their limbs into them. Then before I left the field, I saw a man wearing the next generation of sleeves: a triangular flap that covered the upper arm, not a sleeve at all. Chip Morris (2010) has documented such changes in highland Chiapas, where the rhythm of innovation has accelerated from a new design of outfit every year for the fiesta to a new design at least twice a year with ever more drastic changes.

The same processes affect oral literature. Once upon a time people learned the stories and how to tell them in informal contexts, boys with men together in the fields, girls with women at the hearth or collecting firewood, and both in long candle-lit evenings with the family. Good storytellers were a primary source of entertainment. I remember occasions on which I would ride in the back of a truck with the other passengers on the three-hour trip to and from Chenalhó and San Cristóbal de Las Casas. If we were lucky the Chenalhó butcher would be on the truck, and he could spin story after story to form a narrative that lasted all the way to our destination.

Now a lot of the contexts in which stories were told no longer exist. Children go to school to learn a different genre of stories, and home entertainment may involve books or a radio or television rather than an elder. One effect of the loss of context is the decline of indigenous botanical knowledge; children learn rudimentary Western botany in schools but not the plants in their environment. The effect of this cultural and social change can also be seen in government-sponsored collections of stories in indigenous languages. Tales told by younger speakers often seem to take comic books as their literary models, not traditional narratives. (For a sample of published texts in one Mayan language, see the inventory of Chol narratives in Josserand et al. 2003 and Hopkins and Josserand 2016.)

Countering this acculturative tendency is another factor. In the latter half of the twentieth century, a number of programs were founded with the goal of training speakers of indigenous languages to carry out research on their own languages. In Guatemala, for instance, the Programa Lingüístico Francisco Marroquín in Antigua; in Mexico the Programa de Etnolingüística in Pátzcuaro (and later elsewhere). These and similar programs have produced a cadre of native linguists who are closer to their traditions than any outsider could be, and to a certain extent they have contributed to the preservation of native lore (see Vásquez 2001). However, time is limited, and what is not collected while more traditional storytellers are still alive is lost. It would truly be a shame if feeble efforts like the present work were the only remains of an impressive tradition of narrative art.

Discourse Structures of the Narratives

The more traditional of these narratives display a structure familiar to me from Chol folktales (Hopkins and Josserand 2016), but with notable differences. Narrators tend to open their talk with what has been called an evidentiality statement, brief remarks about where the story comes from—on what evidence does the storyteller relate the events? More traditional folktales may be attributed to the ancestors: *Ay wal jun yik'ti' ko mam kicham chi' ay kanih,* There is a story of our ancestors that remains (Coyote and Rabbit). The narrator may cite a more recent source: *Ay jun toto wab'nak*, There is one I just heard (Friend of the Animals). The story may simply be relegated to the distant past: *Ha' t'ay pekatax ay jun winh icham chi'*, A long time ago there was an old man (An Old Man Whose Son Killed Him). In any case, we are told that this is not something the narrator him or herself witnessed but part of the oral literature. In contrast, a personal narrative or a general discussion of things present begins quite differently: *T'a jun k'uh tik, ol wala' chajtil skutej sk'eta ats'am ats'am*, Today, I'll talk about how we bring up the salt (Taking Out the Salt). The historical account of The Sorcerer begins: *Antonse swik'ti'ej winh anima chi', porke tob' te aj b'al winh*, So, people talk about a man, because he was a great sorcerer. These attributions to one's own knowledge or community lore are the equivalent of the evidentiality statement.

After the opening evidentiality statement, necessary background information is supplied to set the scene for what follows. This may be brief: *ay jun tsanh yuninal winh, tsijtum yuninal winh chi'*, He had some sons, he had many sons (An Old Man Whose Son Killed Him). It may be longer (Friend of the Animals):

Yuj chi',	So,
aj k'ol jun winh t'a junxo winh . . .	one man was the enemy of another . . .
Haxo winh chi' te ijan'och winh t'a winh.	He was always demanding things.
Ah, taktob' te muy wena jente	They say he was a very good man.
jun winh chi'	
Haxob' syalan winh jun to . . .	So they said about one man . . .
ah, te wenaj te wen omre winh chi'.	such a good man that man was.
Haxob' jun winh chi' chuk sk'ol winh.	The other man had an evil heart.

In the long historical narrative The Sorcerer, the background segment runs to nearly twenty percent of the text before the use of the completive aspect marker *ix* signals the first event on the event line: *Entonse, hanheja' chi', ix yab'an heb' winh, jantak heb'winh chuk chi jun*, So, just like that, they heard, many of those powerful men.

The background having been set, narration of a traditional tale proceeds to the event line, the framework around which the story unfolds. In the discourse style of the Chol, events on the event line are related in the completive aspect, like the example just cited in the Chuj story of The Sorcerer. But such is not the case in many of the present tales. Some contain not a single instance of the completive aspect. They are related in a timeless past, but there are other elements that place the events of the narrative in nonpresent times. One such marker is the reportative, appearing in various forms: *hab',-ab'*, or simply-*b'*, which I have usually glossed "they say." Identifying the events of the story as traditional knowledge places them in the past without the need for further marking. The avoidance of the completive aspect also makes the point that the events are not something that we can say actually took place at some specified time (unless they did). In the present set of texts, events as such tend to be heavily weighted with quoted dialogue. If the narrator is able to quote dialogue, the implication is that the events really did take place. Furthermore, the use of dialogue makes the actors real in a way that descriptive prose would not.

A series of related events, usually taking place in the same setting and with the same protagonists, makes up an episode. Each single event may be introduced by its own particular background segment that changes the scene or the actors in some way. A new event may be introduced by one of the standard introductory words (*yuj chi', entonse, yos, weno*, and so forth [for that reason, then, yes, okay]). The last event of an episode may be closed out in a couplet (reminiscent of the scene-closing couplets in Shakespeare's plays). In Friend of the Animals, for instance, the events end with sentences coupled either by the main narrator or by him and the secondary narrator. This back-channeling is typical of tales told in a natural setting, where there are narrators and listeners all participating in the discourse. The full set of event closings in Friend of the Animals is the following (DGA and PSP are the two storytellers):

DGA: *B'at heb' winh, b'i'an.*	They went, then.
PSP: *B'at heb' winh.*	They went.
PSP: *Yak'anxi alkansar spat nok'.*	He was able to get home again.
K'och chi nok' t'a spat chi jun.	The dog went back to his home.
PSP: *Tsab' yik'anb'at ixim nok'*	Those fish carried the maize away.
chay chi'.	
DGA: *Nok' chay chi'.*	Those fish.
PSP: *"K'inalokam yoch wejel t'a ko k'ol*	"Every day they get hungry like we
tik," xab'ih.	do," they say he said.
DGA: *Hi'.*	Yes.
DGA: *T'a winh yuk'tak chi'.*	Against his brother.
PSP: *Hi', t'a winh uk'tak chi'.*	Yes, against the brother.

PSP: *Yak'an hab' b'at jun yol sat winh.*   They say he gave him one of his eyes.
Yo, masanto yak'b'at jun yol sat winh.   Yes, he even gave him one of his eyes.

PSP: *Kan winh.*   The man stayed behind.
DGA: *B'at winh chi' b'i'an.*   That (other) man left, then.

PSP: *Sb'oxi winh, b'i'an.*   The man was well again, then.
DGA: *B'oxi winh, b'i'an.*   The man was well again, then.

At the very end of a narration, there is usually a closing phrase that tells the listeners that the story has ended. There is no more to come. This may be as simple as *Ix lajwih*, It ended (An Old Man Whose Son Killed Him, The Sorcerer). Friend of the Animals was a tale told by two narrators that began with one saying he had just heard a story and that the other man knew it. It ends with a jubilant cry: *Weno, na'an ku'uj!* Okay, we remembered it!

In the narratives that are not traditional folktales, there is less formal structuring. They do tend to begin with an opening, something like an evidentiality statement if just an announcement of what is to come: *Swik'ti'ej winh anima chi'*, I'll tell about a man . . . (The Sorcerer); *Walb'at ha tik ne'ik, ol walb'atih, walelta chajtil ix k'ulej . . .*, I will speak now, I will speak out, about how we did (The Communists); *T'a jun k'uh tik, ol wala'. . . .* Today, I will talk about . . . (Taking Out the Salt).

Following the opening, there may not be a clear set of events organized into episodes, and background information may be mixed in with what amounts to the event line. However, the narration will be segmented into paragraph-like sections by introductory words like *yuj chi'*, *entonse* and *yos*. In the transcription of these nontraditional narrations, I have added marginal notes that mark major changes in topic; in an oral presentation, pauses and alterations of vocal quality are used for the same purpose.

At the end of the narration, the narrator may recap the events or comment on them in some way (parallel to what we have called the denouement in Chol folktales): *Yuj chi', icha chi', chamnak winh anima chi'. . .*, So, in that way, the man died (The Sorcerer); *Icha chi' ix ko k'ulej t'a jun tiempo chi'*, Thus we did in that time there (The Communists); *Yuj chi', icha chi' yet'nak yik ats'am ats'am chi'*, So, that's the way it is with the salt (Taking Out the Salt). Texts normally then close with some device that tells the listener(s) that the performance is over: *Weno, ix lajwih*, Okay, it's over. Turn off the recorder.

The observation that traditional folktales are narrated in a more structured way than personal or procedural narratives emphasizes the point that there is a narrative tradition that has norms, an oral literary canon. This tradition goes back a long way. Based on our understanding of current narrative practices, we have been able to identify their antecedents in Classic period hieroglyphic texts. While the substance of the discourse markers may have changed, the structures they participate in are more resilient. The overall structures of formal texts are similar, as are the rhetorical devices employed. A comparison of two essays by the late Kathryn Josserand is instructive. In one (Josserand 1991), she described the literary patterns of Classic hieroglyphic texts at Palenque. In another (Josserand 2016), she provided a parallel discussion of the patterns of modern Chol storytellers. Others have made similar observations about the continuity of literary aspects of Mayan culture (see Hull and Carrasco 2012 for an excellent sample drawn from Classic, Colonial, and modern material). Not only do the modern Maya have a rich oral tradition; their remote Classic ancestors had standards of literature that deserve to be recognized along with their achievements in art, architecture, astronomy, and calendrics.

CHAPTER 3

Coyote and Rabbit

THIS TEXT HAS SEVERAL interesting aspects. In the opening evidentiality statement the story is attributed to the ancestors, although it can clearly be argued that it is imported, parallel to the African story cycle known to Americans as the tales of Br'er Fox and Br'er Rabbit (see Diarassouba 2007 for an Ivory Coast version, featuring Hyena and Rabbit). On the one hand, tales of Rabbit Trickster are common in the Americas. On the other hand, the introduction (in episodes not reported here but included in the oral text posted on AILLA) of foreign artifacts like cheese and the tar baby mark this story as not entirely native in its origins. The use of Spanish loanwords for the names Rabbit and Coyote also suggests a non-native origin.

This story was recorded in San Mateo Ixtatán in May 1965. Francisco Santizo Andrés and I were there to begin a dialect survey of Chuj-speaking communities, taking advantage of the weather. It was the end of the dry season, and on the climb out of town when we started our two-week trek we encountered one of the daykeepers assuring a man coming down to the market that the rains were sure to come in the next few days. In fact they came as we were returning to San Mateo a fortnight later. We had arrived in San Mateo in the morning of May 1, and Francisco was spending some well-deserved time with his family. I was housed in the municipal offices in the small plaza facing the church. Francisco came and went as he tried to contract beasts of burden for our trip, with little success. Friends dropped by to see him, and we elicited a set of questionnaires and a matching census during the morning. In the evening we were again visited by a number of Francisco's friends and acquaintances, and one of them, Baltazar Tomás, from the aldea Patalcal, dictated this story.

A text that I recorded the next day, from a near-monolingual Chuj speaker, was Oedipus Rex (here called An Old Man Whose Son Killed Him). The tale was complete to the riddle about what animal walks first on four legs, then two legs, and finally three legs (Man). These stories from the international repertory must have been taught at some time in the local schools. Good stories do get around. A Jacaltec version of this Coyote-Rabbit tale was published by Grine-vald (Craig 1978).

Lexical Issues

The term for "ancestors," *ko-mam k-icham*, is in itself interesting; it is a compound noun formed by the juxtaposition of two possessed kin terms, *mam* "father," and *icham* "uncle/nephew" (father's brother, mother's brother, and reciprocal, sibling's son; Hopkins 2012a). This metonymic union of two opposing categories implies the immediately inclusive superior category, in this case, "male ancestors," including both direct and collateral relatives. Note that the corresponding term for ancestors in Ch'ol is *lak tyatyña'älob*, "our father-mothers" based on *tyaty-ña'* "father-mother."

It is notable that the Rabbit is treated distinctly from the other animals mentioned. Chuj has a set of "noun classifiers" that function both as determinatives and as pronouns (Hopkins 1967a, 2012b; see the appendix). Here, Rabbit is honored with the marker for "male (human)," *winh*, while the other protagonists are demoted to *nok'*, "animal": *winh konejo, nok' koyote*, although the narrator occasionally mixes the noun classifiers up and says *nok' konejo* or *winh koyote*. The early protagonist Ram carries the special animal-class designation for horn-bearing mammals, *ch'ak*: *ch'ak kalnel*. Curiously—or perhaps another indication of the foreign origin of the story—the protagonists take Spanish loanword names *konejo, koyote,* and *kalnel* (from *conejo, coyote,* and *carnero*). Rabbit is never called by his native name, *chich*. Coyote appears first as native *okes*, but the narrator later switches to introduced *koyote*. There is no native equivalent for the name of the introduced mammal *kalnel*.

Overview

The episodes of the narration consist of a descriptive passage and a dialogue, terminating in a closing event. This pattern repeats three times before transiting to the following episode (not reported here). The text opens with an evidentiality statement.

Opening: There is a story.
Evidentiality: Our ancestors told it.
First Event
    Background: The Ram is introduced, then the Coyote.

Dialogue: Coyote asks if Ram has seen his friend Rabbit. Ram responds that he is over by that boulder. Coyote says he'll go there.

Closing: Coyote leaves.

Second Event

Background: Coyote finds Rabbit pushing on a boulder shrouded by swirling clouds.

Dialogue: Coyote hails Rabbit. Rabbit tells him his story. Coyote responds he will help.

Closing: Rabbit leaves, and Coyote stays, thinking he is holding up the rock.

Third (Peak) Event

Background: Coyote lets go of the rock, which doesn't fall. He has been tricked.

Dialogue: Coyote swears vengeance on Rabbit (in coupleted lines).

Closing: Coyote leaves.

The peak event of this episode is marked as such by the structure of the dialogue (or monologue). Coyote speaks in parallel statements, a couplet followed by a triplet. (Note that the verb Coyote uses to voice his suspicions is the Spanish loanword *joder*.)

The story continues through a number of such episodes, all with similar structures: Coyote comes up on Rabbit in a situation that is described, they engage in conversation, and Rabbit tricks Coyote and escapes; Coyote follows swearing vengeance. After the rock outcrop incident, Coyote comes upon Rabbit seated on a stump in a clearing, eating a potato, which he shares with Coyote. Coyote asks where he got it, and Rabbit informs him that we all have them, hanging between our legs. Coyote sees that that is the case, and asks how he can get them out of their container. The way to get them is to sit down on the stump and smash them with a rock, says Rabbit, and he departs while Coyote is raising a large rock to smash his testicles. Coyote comes upon Rabbit staring at the reflection of the moon in a stream, Rabbit tells him it is a cheese that can be had only if Coyote drinks the water it lies beneath; while Rabbit escapes, Coyote drinks so much water he swells up and bursts. Coyote comes upon Rabbit in a garden where the farmer has set out a tar baby to catch marauders, Rabbit tricks Coyote into attacking the tar baby, and escapes while Coyote is stuck to the tar. In the final episode in this telling, Rabbit tricks Coyote into falling into a farmer's trap and departs.

A somewhat different version of the Coyote and Rabbit story has found its way to the neighboring Kanjobalan language Jacaltec (Grinevald 1978). A priest annoyed that Rabbit has taken a bite out of his watermelon sets a "tar baby" trap—a wax cross—and snares the villain. Before he can return with a hot wire to run up Rabbit's anus, Coyote appears and is tricked into getting stuck. Rabbit escapes and Coyote pays the penalty. Rabbit then tricks Coyote with the "falling" rock, followed by the cheese in the water and finally the fruit-between-the-legs, in this case, the seeds of the *coyol* tree. Unlike the Chuj story, Coyote's attempt to extract the seeds proves fatal.

It is notable that these episodes have the classic structure of the "short con," as described by David Maurer (1940) in *The Big Con*. In the short con, the swindler takes the victim for an immediate reward, whatever he has with him; in the "big con," the victim is sent off to bring back even more goodies. In both, the con man sets up a situation that attracts the attention of the potential victim. He then "tells him the tale" (in this case that the boulder is about to fall and kill them). The victim falls for it, and the con man "takes the touch," receives his reward (here, escape). The con man must somehow "cool out" the victim and escape (in this case convincing the coyote to stay holding up the boulder). The con man moves on to another victim. In this extended tale, Rabbit fools the same victim, Coyote, over and over again.

Grammatical Notes

Unlike many other Mayan tales, this narration does not make use of the contrast between incompletive (ongoing) and completive (finished) aspects of the verb. Chol, for instance, uses the former for background information and the latter for the event line (Josserand 2016). Here, the event line is related in noncompletive forms. Quoted dialogue uses all aspects, but the encapsulating text does not. However, the events are shown to have happened in the past by the use of the reportative particle *hab'*, glossed here "they say" (and reduced to *-ab'* or even *-b'* in verbal constructions). This particle is used to mark statements that are traditional knowledge, not current events or hearsay but things that happened long ago and are known only from the oral tradition. At the end of the opening evidentiality statement, the past status of the actions to be related is indicated by the adverb *peka'*, "long ago":

> *Ay wal jun yik'ti' komam kicham chi' aykanih.*
> There is a story from our ancestors which remains.
> *Hab' yak' jun tsanh komam kicham chi' peka'.*
> They say some of our ancestors gave it [to us] long ago.

The sentences that enclose the reported dialogue are marked with the reportative *hab'*, *-ab'*, *or -b'*). For instance, in the first, long passage, the reportative appears only in the initial sentence (*ayab'*):

Ayab' nok' ch'ak kalnel. They say there was a ram.

Following the quoted speech by the coyote and introducing the speech of the ram, the reportative appears once again, and again in the closing of the quote (*Haxob' . . . xchab'*):

Haxob' yalan nok' ch'ak kalnel chi' t'a nok' okes chi', t'a nok' koyote chi' . . .
　　They say that ram spoke to that coyote, to that Coyote . . .
. . . xchab' nok' kalnel chi', t'a nok' koyote chi'.
　　. . . said, they say, that Ram to that Coyote.

Coyote responds and leaves, ending the first event. Coyote goes off to find Rabbit, and his greeting is again marked with the reportative particle (*yawajab'*):

Antonse sk'anb'an, yawajab' b'at, haxo winh konejo chi' jun.
　　Then he asked, he cried out, they say, to that Rabbit, then.

Rabbit is leaning against a rock concealed by swirling clouds, pushing against it with his hands, reportedly (*hab'*):

La'an chab'il hab' sk'ab' jun konejo chi',
la'an yamjinak jun k'e'en chi'.
　　Propped by two, they say, hands of Rabbit,
　　propped was held that rock.

Coyote's greeting is again marked by the reportative (*xchab'*):

"Tas tsa k'ulej chi', konejo," xchab' nok' koyote chi'.
　　"What are you doing there, Rabbit?" they say said that Coyote.

And when Rabbit has finished his explanation, the reportative appears again (*xchab'*):

"Sta wyen," xchab' nok' koyote chi'.
　　"Okay," they say that Coyote said.

When the coyote discovers he has been tricked, his final speech is again marked as reported (*xchab'*):

. . . xchab' winh koyote chi'.
     . . . they say Coyote said.

The reportative particle appears throughout the episode to place the events in the distant past, known only from the oral tradition. Thus without employing the completive aspect (something that definitely happened and is finished) the story is marked as an ancient affair.

The use of the reportative instead of the completive aspect may also suggest that these events are not concrete events that took place at specific times (the completive aspect) and not on-going actions in recent or current time (the incompletive aspect), but are timeless mythological events.

Coupleting Marks the Peak Event

The coyote's monologue that ends the final episode consists of a couplet and a triplet, the "zone of turbulence surrounding the peak" (Longacre 1985):

"Tob'an tonhej tsin yak' joder winh,
tob'an tonhej tsin yak' joder winh konejo tik."
     Maybe he's just screwing me,
        maybe this Rabbit is just screwing me."
Tak olin lajelih.
Tak tekan to, olin mila'.
To olin say hin k'olok.
     Perhaps I will finish him.
     Perhaps still I will kill him.
     Still I will look for my enemy.

Exit Coyote. Curtain down. End of the first act.

Coyote and Rabbit

Narrator: Baltazar Tomás, of Patalcal, San Mateo Ixtatán, Huehuetenango, Guatemala

Recorded in San Mateo Ixtatán, May 1, 1965

Chuj Text 26 [CAC 002 R027] (Text IV in Hopkins 1967a)

This transcription covers only the first in a series of episodes; after the rock incident, the rabbit fools the coyote with a series of tricks, including one having to do with a potato (in which the coyote smashes his testicles, having been told that is how to get a tasty potato), one involving the moon's reflection in water looking like a cheese (in which the coyote drinks an entire river to get at the "cheese" under the water, and explodes), an incident in a cabbage patch (in which the coyote gets stuck to the tar baby), and finally, the coyote is lured into a Ladino's trap. (Morphological and syntactic analysis in appendix 2.)

	[Opening]
Chi tik (tik) ha wal jun yik'ti'al yaj.	Well, there is a story.
	[Evidentiality Statement]
Ay wal jun yik'ti' ko mam kicham chi'	There is a story of our ancestors
ay kanih.	that remains.
Hab' yak' jun tsanh ko mam	They say some ancestors did this
kicham chi',	
peka'.	a long time ago.
	[First Event]
	[Background]
Ayab' nok' ch'ak kalnel.	There was, they say, a ram.
Ay wanok mam ch'ak kalnel.	There was an old ram.
Xch'okoj nok' sb'ey t'a jun b'e chi'.	He was walking alone on a road.
Chaan el sb'a nok' ch'ak kalnel chi'	The ram met
jun okes.	a coyote.
Antonse	Then,
t'a yem xo k'uhalil chaanab' el sb'a	Late in the day, they say, met
jun okes chi' yet' jun ch'ak kalnel chi'.	that coyote with the ram.
	[Dialogue]
Xal tik neik:	Here, now:
"Ke, ch'ak kalnel.	"You, Ram!
To tsin k'anb'ej t'ayach,	I ask you,
mama b'aj ix híl	is there anywhere you've seen

winh wamigu, (winh) winh konejoh.
To ay janik' junin tarate yet' winh.
To tarate swilin b'a yet' winh
t'a b'aj ay jun k'en,
jun k'en nha k'e'en,"
chab' nok' okes chi'
t'a nok' kalnel.
Bwenoh.
Haxob' yalan nok' ch'ak kalnel chi'
t'a nok' okes chi jun,
t'a nok' koyote chi',
"Ix wil winh,
hatik aykan ek' winh
t'a jolom lum wits chi',
t'a tsalan chi'.
Hata' ay winh,
t'a yich jun te niwan taj.
Hata' ayek' winh
t'a b'ajay jun k'en tenam chi'.
Tanhwab'il ha k'ochih,"
xchab' nok', nok' kalnel chi',
t'a nok' koyote chi'.

Bwenoh.
"Heh, b'at wil winh an chi'."
B'at kan jun ch'ak kalnel chi'.
Entonse xcha'ankan b'e nok' okes.

B'at nok', k'och nok'
t'a b'ajtil ayek' winh konejo chi'.
Haxob' yílan winh (winh) konejo jun.
To k'och winh koyote.
Antonse sk'anb'an yawajab' b'at,
haxo winh konejo chi jun.
Chek'anoch winh
t'a jun icham tenam chi'.
To lanhan sb'at asun.

my friend Rabbit?
I have a date with him.
A date to meet him
by a cave,
a shelter cave,"
they say the coyote said
to the sheep.
Well.
Then, they say, the ram said
to that coyote,
to the *coyote*.
"I saw him.
He is over there
on top of that mountain,
on that ridge.
He is there
at the foot of a big pine tree.
He is there
where there is a large boulder.
He is waiting for your arrival,"
they say that ram said
to that coyote.
[Closing]
Well.
"Well, I'll go see him, then."
The sheep left.
Then the coyote took the trail.
[Second Event]
[Background]
He left, and arrived
where the rabbit was standing.
Then, they say, he saw the rabbit.
Coyote arrived.
Then he cried out
to Rabbit there.
He was standing leaning
on a big boulder.
The clouds were swirling thickly.

To lanhan sb'at asun
t'a spatik k'en,
yuj chi' to skotkan k'e'en.
Entonse,
ijan och la'an
chab'il hab' sk'ab' jun konejo chi',
la'an yamjinak jun k'e'en chi'.
Ayuch nok' yoyalok k'e'en.
Hi' to wan skotan yib'anh,
sna'anih.

Wenoh.
"Tas tsa k'ulej chi', konejoh,"

xchab' nok' koyote chi'.
Sk'och nok' koyote t'a nok' konejoh.
"Malaj. Kotanh ak' pawor!
Ochanh kan t'atik.
Yam kan jun k'e'en tik!
To chi' ijan skot k'e'en.

Pero tik niwan hach,
ay hip.
Ichamom ha te'el.
A, ol hak' yet'ok.
Tik yam kanih!
B'atin say chab'ok koy.
To ka te oy kak'kanoch t'atik,
yik manh ol lanhchaj jun k'e'en tik,"
xchab' nok' konejo chi' t'a nok'
koyote chi'.
"Sta wyen," xchab' nok' koyote chi'.

Yoch kan ijan nok' koyote chi'.
Hi, yoch kan wetz'wetz'
t'a jun tenam chi'.
Lanhan sb'ey asun.

The clouds were swirling thickly
about the surface of the rock,
so it seemed to move forward.
Then,
leaning, pressing,
both hands of that rabbit, they say,
were grabbing against that rock.
Like he was propping it up.
Yes, the rock was falling over,
he thought.
[Dialogue]
Well.
"What are you doing
there, Rabbit?"
they say the coyote said.
The coyote drew near the rabbit.
"Nothing. Come do me a favor!
Come stay here.
Grab this rock!
The thing is, the rock is
falling over.
But, here, you are big,
you are strong.
You are tall.
You can handle it.
Grab hold here!
I'll go look for a couple of props.
Then we'll put the props here
so this rock doesn't fall over,"
the rabbit said to the coyote.

"OK," the coyote said.
[Closing]
The coyote stayed there.
Yes, he stayed there pushing
against the boulder.
The clouds swirled thickly about.
[Third (Peak) Event]

Ke, te k'itax chi',
ayxom junok ora
sb'at nok' (nok') konejo chi',
(tek'b'anh) tek'tek' wal
aj winh (winh) koyote chi'.
Yel nhilnaj winh
t'a yalanh k'en tenam,
sna'anih
yem kan naynaj jun tenam chi',
sna'an winh koyote chi'.
Tik ni malaj k'en tenam chi' telwih.
Hanheja' yaj k'e'en.
Hi', malaj ik'an k'en.

Wenoh.
"Tob'an tonhej tsin yak' joder winh.
Tob'an tonhej tsin yak' joder
winh konejo tík.

Tak olin lajelih.
Tak tekan to,
olin mila',
to olin say hin k'olok,"
xchab' winh koyote chi'.

B'atchi winh.

[Background]
Later,
about an hour
after the rabbit left,
stood up straight
the coyote.
He leaped out
from under the boulder.
He thought
the boulder would fall down!
The coyote thought that.
But the boulder didn't fall.
The stone just stood there.
Yes, nothing happened to
the stone.
[Dialogue (Peak)]
[Couplet]
Well.
"Maybe he's just screwing me.
Maybe just screwing me
is Rabbit.
[Triplet]
Maybe I'll finish him.
Maybe
I'll kill him.
"If I find him, I'll eat him!"
they say Coyote said.
[Closing]
And he went away again.

CHAPTER 4

An Old Man Whose Son Killed Him

O N MAY 1, 1965, Francisco Santizo Andrés and I left our headquarters in Huehuetenango to start a dialect survey of Chuj from a base in San Mateo Ixtatán. The trip was made in a bus owned by the Argueta company; the alternative was the Osiris bus that left a little earlier. Departure times were around 3 a.m., much earlier than necessary. It seems the two bus companies had been competing for passengers by each trying to leave a little earlier than the other, and they had finally hit a limit beyond which passengers would not go. By dawn we had climbed thousands of feet, and we stopped at a roadside eatery near the turn for Todos Santos Cuchumatán for a warming cup of coffee. We arrived in San Mateo at 10:30 a.m., shortly before Osiris, and the two buses went on to Barillas, where there was a fiesta, Santa Cruz, the day we arrived. This was also the day of the official inauguration in Barillas of the highway, Guatemala Highway No. 9, and the opening of two schools there.

I secured housing in the municipal building, a room next door to the treasurer's office, at the end of the building next to the market. During the day this room was being used as an office by a commission from the Instituto Nacional de Transformación Agraria, receiving some twenty men who supplied data on residences and their families for purposes of securing titles to unused land, similar to the ejido system in Mexico. Francisco was busy making arrangements for our travel. Because of the fiesta in Barillas, there was a shortage of mules in San Mateo, and we could only secure two animals, a mule and a horse. In the evening Francisco visited with friends and we recorded a folktale, the Coyote-Rabbit tale included in this collection.

Sunday, May 2, we took advantage of the number of people coming into the market and took wordlists and one census. A paired set of census and wordlist came from a local man from the cantón of Yune Chonhab' (Little San Mateo), located below the Calvario ruins. The other wordlist was with a man from Patalcal originally from San Sebastián Coatán. In the evening we recorded conversations and storytelling with other people. One of the stories we recorded is this text. I didn't pay too much attention to the contents of the story; our routine was that Francisco would interview the Chuj speaker while I handled the tape recorder (or otherwise transcribed). My attention was on recording level and other technical aspects, not on what the speaker was saying. In this case the speaker was Pascual García Antonio, a native of San Mateo; an unidentified man made occasional comments, not all of which are transcribed here (but see the indented text within parentheses for substantive interventions).

Back in Huehuetenango in mid-May after field work, we dedicated ourselves to processing the material we had recorded. Francisco did all of the transcription from tape, and would bring me a text after he had a transcription of the Chuj and a rough translation to Spanish. I would go over the text and the translation and prepare a translation into English, add the lexical data to my slip files, and prepare questions about the grammar for later sessions. As soon as I started on this text, titled An Old Man Whose Son Killed Him, I realized what it was, a version of Oedipus Rex, told in Chuj by a near monolingual speaker, and presented as a traditional tale, as indicated by the opening, *ha t'ay pekatax ay jun winh icham chi'*. . . . "A long time ago there was an old man. . . ." There are numerous clues that this story is not native in origin, but it is well assimilated.

This text has a much more twisted history than the others presented here. Since it had special interest, I separated it from the other texts, intending to prepare it as a single article. This never got done, and over the years I lost all but the English translation and the tape recording. When I returned to work on the Chuj narratives in 2017, I first attempted a new transcription of the tape (now a digital file, courtesy of the Archive of the Indigenous Languages of Latin America). So much of the recorded text was delivered in a quick and colloquial style that I could not produce a reliable transcription. I appealed to colleagues for help. A professional translator in Los Angeles never responded to my request. Cristina Buenrostro in Mexico City had just sent her Chuj assistant home. Judie Maxwell at Tulane, another Chujista, suggested I contact Francisco Santizo's brother, now said to reside in Canada, but this contact also failed. Through a friend in San Cristóbal de Las Casas I was put in touch with Elena Delfina Yojcom Mendoza, a teacher in Yalambojoch, and she agreed to try to get the story transcribed. After a few months she apologized for the delay and sent me a transcription and translation to Spanish. When I listened to the recording and tried to follow the transcription, it was clear that the scribe had retold portions of the story when the listening got tough. (It was still a good story, though!) In the meantime I had made contact with Jessica Coon and her team in Montreal, including Justin Royer and Paulina Elias. They took on the job as a training project for a new Chuj colleague, Magdalena Torres. I offered my English translation as a guide, but I was told that English was not one of Magdalena's languages, only Chuj, Spanish, and French. After a few months I received a new transcription (and translation), again with some suspicious segments that I was able to resolve. The version presented here is thus a reconstructed transcription drawn from these various sources, but I believe it is accurate. I took my English translation, done in consultation with Francisco Santizo Andrés in 1965, as basic, added what I could reliably transcribe, and tried to fit into it elements of the two Chuj transcriptions. I listened to the recording over and over, and made some changes (apart from the second speaker's interventions, which were difficult to hear). The result may not be a perfect representation of the original oral text, but it is as close as any transcription can be expected to be, and it is certainly the case that the story could have been told this way!

The diviner consulted by the new father is here called *winh ja'at* and *winh xchumum*. The former is based on *ja'at*, the act of making traditional ceremonies (see the agentive noun *jatum*, prayermaker, Academia de Lenguas Mayas de Guatemala 2003:41). The latter is based on the noun *chum*, the hard red fruit of the tropical tree by the same name, probably *Erythrina* species (Hopkins 2012a). Another name for the specialists who cast fortunes with these bean-like fruits is *aj chum*, "master of the beans." The beans are laid out in arrays related to the part of the ancient Mayan calendar that combines numbers one to thirteen with twenty day names, creating 260 meaningful combinations. A person's fate is in part determined by the date of birth and the combination of forces that prevailed over that date. This and other techniques of divination have been described by a number of ethnographers (see Colby and Colby 1981 for a detailed discussion of this tradition among the Ixil; see Bassie-Sweet 2008:92–96 for further references and discussion).

It is suggested in the text that the game in which the young man gets involved was *bras*. This is a loanword from Spanish *barajas*, and refers to games played with the Spanish deck of fifty cards also called *naipes* that has the suits *copas, bastones, espadas*, and *oros* (corresponding to hearts, clubs, spades, and diamonds). This is the standard deck for card games in rural Guatemala and Chiapas. The "riddle" that the young man is asked to solve is called *preba*, a loanword from Spanish *prueba*, a "test" or "proof."

There are two comments in the text that are hard to explain. At the end of the episode in which the young man kills the man he has been playing cards with is the statement *Entonse sk'exek'nak winh*. My Guatemalan transcriber skipped this phrase and my Canadian colleague treated it as *sk'exek' naj winh*, "Entonses ahí terminó él" (then there he ended), which is logical but doesn't match the morphology of the verb phrase. There is an honorific *naj* for younger males, used with names, that is, *naj Petul* "young Pedro" (Hopkins 2012a:222). However, if the transcription is correct, this is the only instance of it in this text. I believe the transcription to be *sk'exek'nak winh*, the possessed participle of a verb *k'ex-ek'-(ih)*. The root *k'ex* means "to exchange, replace" and is one of the terms that refers to the replacement of one cargo-holder by another and the substitution of one generation by another (Mondloch 1980). One's *k'exul* is one's namesake (Spanish *tocayo* [from Nahuatl]); children are often named after their grandparents, as they are to become the "replacement of their ancestors. The suffixed directional verb *–ek'* refers to "passing by." The term *k'ex-ek'-nak*, then, should be something like "replacement in passing." That is, the young man *replaced* the older man (in the succession of generations). This makes sense if we know (as we do) that the young man is the son of the older man. This suspicion is reinforced by the second curious comment. Near the end of the text, the suicide of the young man is reported as *ix cham winh smam winh, xcham xi winh. Smil sb'a heb' winh*, "his father died, he died as well. They killed each other."

An Old Man Whose Son Killed Him

Narrator: Pascual García Antonio, of Chonhab' (San Mateo Ixtatán)
   Recorded in San Mateo Ixtatán, May 2, 1965
   Chuj Text 21 [CAC 002 R022].

[Opening]

Weno.

Bueno. [OK]
[Background]

Komo ha' t'ay pekatax
ay jun winh icham chi'. [ay
juntsanh . . .]
Ay juntsanh yuninal winh.
Tsijtum yuninal winh chi'.
Hab' xo yalan winh, [ay jun
winh . . .]
ay jun winh yunin winh chi' ix jali.

Once upon a time
there was an old man. [He had
some . . .]
He had some sons.
He had many sons.
They say he said . . . [there was a
man . . .]
. . . that a new son came.
[First Event: Dialogue]
Then he went to ask his destiny.

Entonse, xit' k'ana' jun . . . jun
sb'ehal winh.
"Ha tik ne'ik, olam k'ib' winh
wuninal tik?
Wach'am ol aj winh t'ayin?"
xchi hab' winh.
"B'at hin k'an to ne'ik
schumal winh."
Sb'at winh b'i'an t'a winh ja'at
winh chi'.
Sk'anan xchumum chi'.

"Now, will my son grow up?

Will he be good to me?"
they say he said.
"I will go now to ask his future."

He then went to the prayermaker.

He asked that diviner.
[Closing]

Yalan winh b'i'an,
ha xo winh xchumum chi' yelta,
t'a xchumal winh chi'.
Ay tonam b'aj
ts'el k'och si'an jab'ok heb' winh.

One asks, then,
that diviner to cast
the fortune of that person.
Perhaps there are times when
some truth comes out in what they say.
[Background]

Entonse, sk'och winh b'i'an,
yalan winh,

Well, then, the man arrived,
and he asked,

"Ha jun wunin tik, olam k'ib' winh,
Wach'am winh?"
"Ha jun winh hunin tik, ha winh
[olach...]
olach julan chamok.
Kon el tiempo sk'ib'i winh,
entonse ke kab'al winh
olach chamok,"
xab' winh.
"Wal yel?"
"Toton yel."

Ha' la yune to winh chi'.
Jantakam de...de...*de un año*,
si más...[mas...mas] manto
[manto manto...]
toman nene to winh chi'.
(*Dos años, dos años*)

Yo, yalan winh ix yistsil winh b'i'an.

"Ha tikne'ik, tas skutik
winh junin tik?
Icha tik b'aj yelta t'ahin to
ha winh olin julan chamok.
Mero manh ol yallaj
ko mak'an cham winh.
Mejor to b'at k'ap kam b'at,
aj b'at kam winh yol junok olan,
mato aj b'at pak' kam winh?'
xchab' winh
(winh smam winh unin)
Winh smam winh unin chi'.
(Ha'.)
"Totom ipanam sb'at ni'o,"
xchab' ix chichim,
"yikan ha b'at winh [winh], b'i'an."

[Second Event: Dialogue]
"Will this son of mine grow up?
Will he be a good person?"
"Ah, this son of yours, he [will...]
he is going to shoot you to death.
In time he is going to grow up,
then he is going to shoot you to death."

they say he said.
"Is that true? [the father asked]
"Yes, it's true." [the diviner answered]
[Closing]
And he was still an infant,
He was one year old
if more [...more...] not yet [not
yet...]
but he was still an infant.
(Two years, two years.)
[Background]
So then, the man talked to his wife.
[Third Event: Dialogue]
"Now what are we going to do
with the child?
It has come to me that
he is going to shoot me to death.
Let's not say
that we'll beat him to death.
Better yet go leave him in a pit.
leave him in some hole.
Or where else can I leave him?"
they say he said.
(the father of that child)
The father of that child.
(Ha!)
"Then he has to go!,"
they say the wife said.
"So you have to go."

Sb'at winh.

Sb'at winh icham chi',
Xit' yak'an winh t'a jun montaña,
Ha ta' xit' yak'an winh.
Pero jun montaña chi',
manh yojtakok laj winh icham chi'
tato slak'anil xo chi'
ay jun chonhab', xchi.
Ha xo yak' jun winh icham
walek' winh icham chi' k'atsits,
o pasyal
o t'asam walek' say . . .

say winh t'a jun montaña
ha xo yab'an winh walok jun
unin chi'.

"Unek', unek', unek',"
xchab' jun chi'.
"Aj ix k'oti?,"
xchab' winh icham chi'.
Xit' sayan yilb'at winh b'i'an.
Ha xo yilan winh hichanab'ek'
jun unin chi'.
Ma chekel aj ix k'oti.

Skal yaxlum ayek'i.

(Tonhej xit' yak'an winh icham.)
Tonhej xit' yak'an winh,
spax t'a winh b'i'an.
To ha winh icham chi'
ix sk'anb'ati.
Sk'och t'a spat winh b'i'an.
Yalan winh, "Ay jun portuna
ix wik'a,"

[Closing]
He left.
[Background]
The old man went out.
He went to leave him in the rain forest.
It was there he went to leave the child.
But that wilderness,
the old man didn't know
that nearby it
there was a village, they say.
Then, an old man
was passing by gathering firewood,
or wandering around,
or who knows what he was
looking for . . .
looking for on that mountain
when he heard the child crying.

[Fourth Event: Dialogue]
"Unek', unek', unek',"
they say he was saying.
"Where is that coming from?,"
they say the old man said.
He went and looked around.
Then he saw lying there was
that child.
But it was unknown where he
came from.
There he was in the middle of
the forest.
(The father just went to leave him.)
He just went out to leave him there,
and then he went home.
Then that old man
took him away.
He arrived at his house.
He said, "I've brought a treasure!,"

xchi winh.
Pero winh icham, ni junok
yuninal winh.
Malaj, xchi.

Sk'ib' winh unin chi' b'i'an.
Ha xo t'a k'ib' winh b'i'an.
Wenas wal k'ib' winh unin chi'.
Icham winak aj winh.

Entonses, totonam algo lak'anam
skal jun chonhab' chi'.
Sb'at winh b'i'an . . .
pasear winh, pax winh icham chi'.

Ay jun k'inh ochi,
yoch jun juego t'a b'ajtil.
Mato braj, mato tas jun,
b'aj yak' juego chi' heb' winh.
Entonses wanem heb' winh chi' jun.

Yo, manh yojtakok laj winh
icham chi' jun
tato ha winh yunin winh chi' yet'i
ol . . . ol ya'an tajnel chi'.
Sino ke yojtak winh to,
ix si'um'anel yunin winh chi',
komo malaj sgana winh
xcham winh jun.
(Manh xo tok' ayek' laj winh
sna'an winh.)

Entonses ya'an winh b'i'an,
yoch juego chi'.

Tik ne'ik ha'am winh icham chi',
mas ak'an ganar jun.
Sk'e'en naj kot k'en pistola.

he said.
But that man had not a single child.

None, they say.
[Closing]
Well, that child grew up.
The child grew up there.
The child grew well.
He came to be a man.
[Background]
Then, maybe not far away
lay another village.
He went there . . .
to wander about, he went again.
[Fifth Event: Action]
There was a fiesta starting,
he got into a game over there.
Maybe cards, or whatever;
where they were playing that game.
There they were, playing.
[Closing]
And, that old man didn't know

that it was his child with whom
he . . . he would be playing.
If he had known,
he would have killed him,
because he didn't want to die.

(He didn't know he was still alive.)

[Background]
So there they were,
the game started.
[Sixth Event: Action]
Maybe it was the old man
who won more.
Pistols were drawn.

Fit! Ya'an winh t'a winh.
Fit! Xlajwi winh icham chi'.
Ha t'a elk'och si'al jun . . . [jun jun]
jun spreba winh chi'.
(T'a b'ajtil xintek' sk'an te'.)

Yo, xcham winh b'i'an.
Entonse sk'exek'nak winh,

Yo, hijun lajan nhej ham jun,
yilanab' xi sb'a, ha na [ix ix]
ix snun winh unin chi' jun.
T'o te wach' yilji ix,
una mujera muy simpática.
Tob' anheja kob'es ix ix chi'.
Anheja wach' yilji ix, entonse.

Yalanab' ix jun:
"Ha tik ne'ik to,
ol och chok winh wichmil
komo to ix cham winh wichmil jun.
Pero, tato sna'elta jun preba
heb' winh anima chi'
Wach' tas tsaj yalan heb',
pero ay jun hin preba hahintik.
Ta to sna'elta jun hin preba chi'
heb' winh,
entonse olin yik winh chi',
lo que sea chekel to anima winh.
Nada más sna'elta jun hin preba chi
heb' winh," xchab' ix.
Sk'och winh anima yak' karinyar ix.
"Tsam ha na'elta jun preba chi'?"
Maj sna'elta laj heb' winh.
("Tas yaj jun ha preba chi' jun?")
"Ha' jun hin prewa:
Ay jun nok' nok'
ha sjawi nok', chanhe' yok nok'.

And *ffft!*, he gave it to him.
Ffft! The old man died.
Thus it came to pass . . .
what the diviner had predicted.
(Where he went to ask his fate.)
[Closing]
So, the man died.
Then the young man took his place.
[Background]
So, maybe a little later
he again came across that . . .
the mother of that child [him].
She was very pretty,
an attractive woman.
They say she was like a maiden.
She still looked good, then.
[Seventh Event: Dialogue]
They say she said,
"Now,
I'll start to look for a husband,
since my husband has died.
But, if they can solve a riddle,
those men.
I don't care what they say,
but I have a riddle of mine,
If they solve my riddle,
those men.
then I will take that man,
whatever he looks like.
All he has to do is solve my riddle,"
they say she said.
People came to court her.
"But can you solve this riddle?"
They didn't answer it.
("What is your riddle, then?")
"My riddle is:
There is an animal
who when he comes, he has four feet.

T'a mas sjawi k'uh,
chanhe' yok nok'.
Haxo t'a chim k'uhalil,
chab' nhej yok nok'.
Ha xo t'a k'uhalil,
oxe' xo nhej pax yok nok'.
chab' ix. [Ha . . .]
Entonse max sna'elta laj heb' winh,
"Ma chekel tas jun chi'!"
("Tas ts'elk'och jun chi'?")
"Tas ts'elk'och jun chi'?"

Entonses sna'elta heb' winh, b'i'an.

Bueno,
to ix k'och winh,
sk'och pax heb' winh unin
chi', b'i'an.

"Ma'ay ke keres k'i ko b'ah?

T'a ma'ay, icha wal tik ts'on aji,"
xchab'.
"Pero sk'i nhej ko b'ah
ta to tsa na'elta jun hin preba,
porke ha'in tik,
ay jun hin preba icha tik."
xchab' ix chichim chi.
"Tas jun ha preba chi' jun?,"
Yalan ix: "Ichatik."
"Ah, bueno, entonse ha'in tik jun,
mejor ix hin na'elta,
ke ha'onh tik jun,
Komo ts'on kotoch uninal
chanhe' kok.
Komo yel ts'on he kotkonok'.
Ha xo chim k'uhalil chi' jun,
chab' xo kok, wach' kek'i.

When it is dawn
he has four feet.
At noon,
he has only two feet.
In the afternoon,
the animal just has three feet again,"
they say that she said. [. . .]
Then they didn't guess it.
"Who knows what this is!"
("What does it mean?")
"What does it mean?"
[Closing]
Well, they thought about it.
[Background]
Okay,
then that man arrived also.
that child arrived also, then.

[Eighth Event: Dialogue]
"So, don't you want us to have
each other?
If not, that's the way we'll do it,"
they say he said.
"But we will come together
if you solve my riddle,
because I,
I have a riddle, like this,"
they say the woman said.
"What is your riddle, then?,"
The woman said: "It's like this."
"Well, okay, then I
guess I have solved it.
that it's us, then.
As infants crawling,
we have four feet.
As infants we walk on our four legs.
At mid-day,
we have two legs and we walk well.

Ha xo t'a yem k'uhalil,
icham winak chi' jun,
oxe' xo pax:
ayoch ko k'och."

Kawal yik'ani snun winh!
(Ah.)

Bueno, entonses, ha tik ne'ik, jun,
yab'an wal elta winh b'i'an,
 tis . . . yaj wal . . . tas wal yaj jun
tajtil yaj jun ix jun.

"Tajtil, chaktil aj jun?"
"Ichatik: Yuj chamnak
winh wichmil
komo ha xo winh ek'nak,
ichatik yaji, yelta"
"Entonses haton winh hin
mam chi',"
xchab' winh unin chi'.
Mismo ha winh yak' matar sb'a, yo.
Slajwi howal chi', b'i'an.

(Ix cham winh?)
Ix cham winh smam winh,
xcham xi winh.
Smil sb'a heb' winh,
ay snun winh yik'laj sb'ah.
Ya stá.
Ix lajwi.

In the afternoon,
as old men,
on three legs again:
we use a cane."
[Closing]
Right there he took his mother!
(Ah.)
[Background]
Well, then, now,
he found out how it was,
. . . uh . . . it was . . . what it was, then,
how the woman was.
[Ninth Event: Dialogue]
"How, what is your story?"
"Like this: Because my husband died,

so since he was gone,
it was like this, it's true."
"Then that man was my father!"

they say the boy said.
Then he killed himself, then.
And the difficulty ended.
[Closing]
(He died?)
His father died,
he died too.
They killed themselves.
It was his mother he mated with.
That's it.
It ended.

CHAPTER 5

Friend of the Animals

T HIS STORY WAS RECORDED in San Mateo Ixtatán February 5, 1965. It is told by Pascual Santizo Pérez, a relative of Francisco Santizo Andrés, with help from Domingo Gómez Antonio, another resident of San Mateo. At the time Francisco and I were collecting plants with Dennis Breedlove, and had just spent two days in the area of San Juan Ixcoy, farther south in the Cuchumatanes. Arriving in San Mateo, Dennis and I settled into our quarters in the municipal building and Francisco went home. In the evening he came back with a couple of friends and they told me this tale.

This story has a certain resemblance to Aesop's story Androcles and the Lion, where a man befriends a wounded lion and is later rewarded for his goodness (theme ATU 156 in the revised Aarne-Thompson classification system for folktales; Stith Thompson 1961). But this is not a tale borrowed from the European tradition. There are native Mayan elements that mark it as an independent story. The association between hawks and eyes occurs in the Popol Vuj (Christenson 2007:154–59), a Colonial Quiché document that is a treasure trove of Maya mythology. There the Hero Twins (another set of brothers) shoot a Laughing Falcon with their blowguns. They bring him down with a ball to the eye, and then discover he is bringing them a message from their Grandmother (carried by a louse in the mouth of a toad in the belly of a snake eaten by the falcon, a notorious predator of snakes). The Twins replace the eye with rubber from the ball they are carrying for their upcoming games with the Underworld gods. Since they have cured him, the falcon delivers the message. Reciprocity: harm is compensated, favors are repaid.

The Chuj story features two men, later revealed to be brothers, one good and the other bad. This theme also appears in a Chol folktale (Our Holy Mother; Hopkins and Josserand 2016:41–52), where the men are the sons of the Moon. The older brother is mean and mistreats his younger brother, who ultimately takes revenge: the older brother has climbed high in a tree to take honey from a wild beehive shown to him by his younger brother, but he refuses to share the

52

honey. The younger brother makes gophers out of the beeswax and the animals fell the tree; the older brother is killed in the fall, breaking up into pieces that become dozens of animals. The younger brother becomes the Sun. Thus, in accordance with a widespread Maya theme, evil is punished and good rewarded. In the Chuj story we are not told about the relative age of the brothers, and while the one who is presumably older is in fact mean, the younger brother merely survives. He survives with the aid of a number of animals he has befriended, repeating the theme of rewarding good deeds. Specifically, he has shared food with the animals, and while this leaves him without food for himself and his brother, the gifts establish an imbalance of reciprocity that must be repaid, another widespread Maya theme.

The good brother is described in terms of Spanish loans as *muy wena jente* (*muy buena gente*, a very good person) and *te wen omre* (very much a *buen hombre*, a good man). The mean brother is said to have an evil nature, *chuk sk'ol* (evil [are] his innards). The body part *k'o'ol* (= *k'ol*) includes the contents of the body cavity and is the Chuj equivalent of the heart in European cultures—the center of emotions (Hopkins 2012a:178). That is, he has an evil heart. But the term *k'o'ol* figures prominently in the realm of witchcraft or sorcery: the *aj k'o'ol* (master of the innards) is someone who works against you by attacking your companion spirit, your *chiápah*, essentially your soul. Like the *aj b'a'al*, master of witchcraft, the *aj k'o'ol* is a kind of *chuk winakil* (Spanish *brujo*, witch or warlock, literally an evil person). The *aj b'a'al* (like the Sorcerer in another tale told here) does physical harm rather than spiritual harm.

The older brother appears to have evil intentions with respect to the younger, as he asks himself, "Where can I take this man to?," plotting to leave him somewhere else. The older brother supplies the food they will eat along the way, but the younger brother keeps giving it away! The recipients of this generosity are not randomly chosen animals, but represent three of the four categories of vertebrates in Maya belief. First, he gives maize to a dog, then to some fish, and he gives meat to a hawk. The four classes are defined by locomotion: walkers (mammals), swimmers (fish), flyers (birds), and crawlers (Hopkins 1980a); left out is the latter, the class of reptiles and amphibians. But the younger brother also feeds ants, representing the invertebrates. Eventually the maize gives out, and the older brother gets very angry. He demands retribution in the form of some edible body part. He settles on the eyes, which he eats one by one, and then leaves his brother blind in the woods. But now reciprocity sets in, and the dog appears to lead the blind man to shelter. The hawk arrives and brings eyes to replace those lost. The younger brother is saved.

The overall theme is, then, the repayment of debts, the maintenance of balance in relationships. The younger brother gives away food supplied by his elder, and when the elder needs to be repaid, the charitable brother has to repay the debt, even if it leaves him incapacitated. However, since he has been feeding the animals, they come to pay him back not with food, but with aid and restoration of his sight. Balance is restored on all accounts.

This principle of balanced reciprocity is basic to Maya belief. The leading folk deity is the Earth Lord, variously named as the Earth (*Mundo, Witz-Ak'lik*), Lord of the Mountain (*Aj Witz*), Earth Owner (*Yahval Balamil*), and so forth, and he is attested in the folklore of Mesoamerican groups from Central Mexico to Central America. He is the owner of the natural resources that humans need to exploit to survive. Consequently, a major concern is making petitions and advance payments for resources about to be used (land, animals, plants, and so forth), and making thank offerings after the fact. If reciprocity is not maintained, payment will have to be made in the form of sickness, death, soul loss, and other undesirable conditions. This principle applies to interhuman affairs as well. In the Chol folktale The Messengers (Hopkins and Josserand 2016:115–27), for instance, a messenger is forced by witches to consume human flesh, and he later dies because he took something that didn't belong to him and he has to pay it back.

Balanced reciprocity was also the rule in social structure. In the patrilineal kinship system once practiced by the Maya (Hopkins 1969, 1988, 1991) neighboring families would exchange sons and daughters as marriage partners. Brother and sister of one family would marry sister and brother of the other. In turn, their children would also marry in their time. Since father's sister's and mother's brother's children (cross-cousins) were not of one's own lineage, they were marriageable. Sibling exchange thus continuously tied the families together. Reciprocity again: our women for your men, your women for ours.

Friend of the Animals

Narrators: Francisco Santizo Andrés (FSA), Pascual Santizo Pérez (PSP), and Domingo Gómez Antonio (DGA), all of Chonhab' (San Mateo Ixtatán, Huehuetenango, Guatemala)

   Recorded in San Mateo Ixtatán on February 5, 1965

   Chuj Text 19 [CAC 002 R020]

[Opening]

FSA: . . . chajti'il, t'ay ajtil . . .

FSA: (Tell us) . . . how it was, when . . .

PSP: Pero mantsak yak'laj grawar winh chi ne'ik.

PSP: But he's not recording yet, is he?

FSA: Manto.

FSA: Not yet. . .

. . . t'a yik ay mam kicham pekataxo.

. . . about our ancestors, a long time ago.

[Evidentiality Statement]

PSP: Ay jun, ay jun,
ay jun toto wab'nak
Yojtak winh.

PSP: There is one, there is one . . .
there is one I just heard;
He (Domingo) knows it.

[Background]

Yuj chi', aj k'ol jun winh t'a junxo winh.
Yo, haxob' (tik tik) . . .
Haxo winh chi' te ijan'och winh t'a winh.
A, taktob' te muy wena jente jun winh chi',

So, one man was the enemy of another man.
Yes, he was always . . .
He was always demanding things of him.
Ah, they say that that one man was a very good man.

Haxob' syalan winh jun to (tik tik) . . .
A, (te wenaj) te wen omre winh chi'.
Haxob' jun winh chi' chuk sk'ol winh.

That's what they said about the one man . . .
Ah, such a good man that man was.
That other man was stingy.

[First Event: Dialogue]

Entonse a yal nhej,
"B'aj olin kuchb'ejb'at winh tik,"
xab' winh chi'.
Tonse yalan winh t'a winh jun,

So, he (the other man) just said,
"Where can I take this man to?"
they say he said.
Then he spoke to the first man,

to sb'at winh yet' winh yak' pasyar.
"Konh b'at kak' junh ko pasyar,
t'a te najat.
Tot jun semana wal tsonh b'ati.
To skik' ixim ko'och," xab' winh.

"A, weno."
Niwan hab' aj ixim yoch heb'
winh chi',
sb'at heb' winh.

(DGA:B'at heb' winh b'i'an.
PSP: B'atab' heb' winh,

Yo, haxob' b'at heb' winh chi jun.
Niwan hab' yoch winh chi'.

Haxob' winh chi jun,
ayab' (jun) jun nok' chi'
yilelta winh.
(DGA:Yilelta heb' winh.
PSP: Totonab' wenas ketkon
yek' nok',
wanab' xcham jun nok' ts'i' chi'
yuj wejel.
(DGA: Hi', wejel.
PSP: "A, tas ts'ik'an?
Seguro to wejel ts'ik'an nok'," xi.
Sk'ehab'kot ixim yoch winh,

yak'anab' yoch nok' winh,
íxtob' ta' sb'ohix nok' ts'i' chi'.

(DGA:...nok' b'ehal chi'.
PSP: Yak'anxi alkansar spat nok'.
K'och chi nok' t'a spat chi' jun.

Entonse, a,
tonhej wanab' xchichon b'at,

if he would go on a trip with him.
"Let's go take a trip,
very far away.
For a whole week we'll go,
we'll take maize to eat," they
say he said.
"Ah, alright."
They say [they took] a lot of
maize to eat,
and they set out.
[Closing]
DGA They went, then.)
PSP: They say they went.
[Background]
So, they say those men went out,
they say they had a lot of maize to eat.
[Second Event: Action, Dialogue]
They say that that other man,
they say . . . he saw an animal

DGA: They saw it.)
PSP: They say it was staggering along,

they say the dog was dying of hunger.

DGA: Yes, hunger.)
PSP: "Ah, what's wrong?
Surely he's hungry," he said.
They say out came their maize
provisions,
they say he gave the dog food,
and the dog recovered, right there.
[Closing]
DGA: . . . dog went down the road.)
PSP: He was able to get home again.
The dog went back to his home.
[Background]
Then, ah,
just for that they say he got annoyed,

sk'ol winh chi t'a winh jun,
komo to te wen omre winh chi'.
Entonse...
(DGA: Wen omre winh t'a winh.
PSP: Yo, b'atchi winh.

Haxob' k'och chi winh jun,
"Kak' armerso t'a tik," xab'i.
"Kak' armerso an,"
xab' winh chi' t'a winh.
(DGA: Yak'an almerso heb' winh.
PSP: B'at heb' winh sti jun ha'.
Halxob' nok' chay.
Halxob' xepanab' em ixim
winh yola'.

(DGA: Yola'.
PSP: (ts'acheb'...)
Tsis ja'al swa'an ixim nok' chay chi',

(DGA: Hi', nok' chay chi'.
PSP: "A, tob'an swa' ixim
nok'," xab'i.

Tsab' xepan'em ixim winh.
Tsab' yik'anb'at ixim nok' chay chi'.
(DGA: Nok' chay chi'.

PSP: Weno, cha'kotxi
heb' winh jun,
haxob' t'a b'aj wan swa winh chi',

b'aj syak' armerso heb' winh chi'.
(DGA: Hi'.
PSP: Haxob' nok' sanich.
(DGA: Haxo nok' sik'anb'at ixim.

PSP: Haxob' ts'el ixim sk'ajil chi',
syik'b'at nok' sanich chi'.

the enemy of the man, then,
since that one was such a good man.
Then...
DGA: The good man, to him.)
PSP: Yes, he went on.
[Third Event: Action, Dialogue]
They say when he got to the other man,
"Let's make breakfast here," he said.
"Let's make breakfast, then,"
they say that man said to him.
DGA: They made breakfast.)
PSP: They went to the bank of a creek.
They say there were fish.
They say he crumbled some maize for
them, into the water.

Into the water.)
(they wet...)
So pretty were those fish, eating
the maize.
DGA: Yes, those fish.)
PSP: "Ah, it's true that fish eat
maize," he said.
[Closing]
He threw down more maize.
Those fish carried the maize away.
Those fish.)
[Background]
PSP: Well, they met again,

they say there where that man
was eating,
where they made breakfast.
DGA: Yes.)
PSP: They say there were ants.
DGA: They were picking up
the maize.)
PSP: They say when maize crumbs fell,
the ants carried them off.

Halxo yik'anb'at ixim.
(DGA: *Lo mismo.*

PSP: "Tob'an swa ixim nok'."
Tsab' xepanxi em ixim winh.
(DGA: . . . xi ixim winh.
PSP: "Tato slajwel ixim hoch tik,

antonse manh hana' to swak'
tsin jab'ok t'ach,"
xab' winh yuk'tak winh chi' t'ay.
(DGA: Te kot yowal winh
chi' t'a winh.
PSP: Te kot yowal.
Mas nhej te kot yowal
winh t'a winh.
(DGA: Hi', te kot yowal
winh t'a winh.
PSP: "Weno, pero ob'iltak nok',
(tos) to swa ixim nok' jun.
K'inalokam yoch wejel t'a ko
k'ol tik,"
xab'i.
(DGA: Hi'.

PSP: Weno, lajwi hab'
yak'an almersoh
heb' winh jun.
Sb'atchi heb' winh.

Haxob' k'ochchi winh jun,
ayab' jun . . .
B'at hab' xi heb' jun,
haxob' jun ch'akb'a wal ek' t'urhok
yib'anh heb' winh.
(DGA: Yib'anh heb' winh.
PSP: Winh heb' winh, yo.
(DGA: Hi'.

They carried off the maize.
DGA: The same thing.)
[Fourth Event: Dialogue]
PSP: "It's true they eat maize."
They say he threw down maize again.
DGA: . . . maize again.)
PSP: "If your maize
provisions run out,
then don't think I'm going to give
you anything,"
they say his brother said to him.
DGA: He got very mad at him.)

PSP: He got very mad.
He just got madder at him.

DGA: Yes, he got very mad at him.)

PSP: "Okay, but the poor animals,
they eat maize, too.
Every day they get hungry like we do,"

they say he said.
DGA: Yes.)
[Closing]
PSP: Okay, they finished making
breakfast,
the men.
They went on again.
[Background]
When they arrived again,
they say there was a . . .
They say when they went on again,
there was a hawk flying around
above them.
DGA: Above them.)
PSP: The men, yes.
DGA: Yes.)
[Fifth Event: Dialogue]

PSP: "A, seguro to ay sk'an nok' tik.

Ts'och swejel nok'."
Ayab' schib'ej winh yet'i.
Hab' xchon jun te' yak'k'en winh.
Yo, yik' yem hab' kot jenhnaj

nok' ch'akb'a chi',
yik'an hab' b'at nok'.
(DGA: La ch'akb'a chi'
yem yik'an b'at nok', b'ihan.
PSP: "A, tik swak' tsin jab' hiko',
tik ol wak' pax tsin jab' hoko',"
xab' winh ichatik.
"T'a yik'an hab' jab'xo," xchi
winh chi'.
Weno.
Tonse ichnhejab' ta jun
haxo winh chi' jun
to te ayuch sk'ol winh t'a winh.
(DGA: Hi', ayuch sk'ol
winh t'a winh.
PSP: Yol ay yoch sk'ol winh.
Yol ay sayan mulan b'ah
winh t'a winh.
(DGA: T'a winh yuk'tak chi'.
PSP: Hi', t'a winh uk'tak chi'.

Yos, b'atab' xi winh.

Weno, sk'och winh
t'a b'at hab' xi heb' winh . . .
Yo, haxob' sk'och winh t'a (t'a t'a) . . .

Haxob' sb'at,
weno, b'at hab' xi heb' winh.
Hatik nek an,
k'och hab' wal ijan chi jun.
Hatik ne'ik (tik tik) . . .

PSP: "Ah, surely this animal wants
something.
He's hungry."
They say he had some meat with him.
He held it up on a stick to give to him.
And they say that hawk came down
to get it,

and carried it away, they say.
DGA: That hawk
came down to take it away, then.)
PSP: "Ah, here's something for you,
I'll give you a bit more food, again,"
they say that man said.
"Take a little bit more," the man said.

Okay.
Then, just like that
that other man
became an enemy to him.
DGA: Yes, he became an
enemy to him.)
PSP: He became an enemy.
He was finding more bad things
that man, against the man.
DGA: Against his brother.)
PSP: Yes, against the brother.
[Closing]
So, they left again.
[Background]
Okay, they arrived
at where they say they . . .
Okay, they say they arrived at . . .
(at . . . at) . . .
They say they went,
okay, they say they went on again.
Now,
they say they arrived.
Now . . .

b'at hab' xi heb' winh jun.
Yak'anab' xi chimk'uhal
heb' winh jun
lajwi hab' el ixim yoch winh chi'.
(DGA: Lajwel ixim yoch winh chi'.

PSP: Hatik nek an (tik tik) . . .
"Tom max hak' tsin
jab'ok t'ayin jun,"
xab' winh yuk'tak winh chi' t'ay.
(DGA: Winh yuk'tak winh chi' t'ay.
PSP: "A, inaton swala'.
Ikut nok' nok' chi nek,
tas suj manhtok tsach,
tas suj mantok . . .
(DGA: "Tas suj mantok
tsak' ayuda nok' t'ayach,"
xcham winh,
"T'ayach," cham winh.
PSP: "Hi', tas yuj mantok
syak' ayudar nok' t'ayach," xab'.

"Weno."
"A pero ob'iltak nok'
ix toton swa nok'.
Tom wojtak tato slajwel íxím," xab'i.
"Hatik nek an,
tas juno tsak' t'ayin?
Tom ha hok.
Mato ha junha k'ab' tsak' t'ayin."
"A komo ke toh
ol wak' jun wok t'ayach?
"Antonse mejor yilxom an . . .
lo mejor ha junh yol ha sat
tsak' t'ayin.
Yik ol hil t'a jun xo,"
xab' winh.
Entonse
(DGA: "Tsak' t'ayin," keom!

they went again.
And they say the next
morning, that man,
they say his maize provisions ran out.
DGA: His maize provisions ran out.)
[Sixth Event: Dialogue]
Now then . . .
"Won't you give a little
something to me?"
they say he said to his brother.
DGA: The man's brother said to him.)
PSP: "Ah, I told you.
Bring those animals now,
why don't you . . .
why don't you . . ."
DGA: "Why don't
those animals help you out,"
he probably said.
"For you," he said.)
PSP: Yes, why don't
the animals help you out?" they
say he said.
"Okay."
"Ah, but the poor animals,
they eat, too.
Did I know the maize would run out?"
"Now, then," [said the brother]
"What are you going to give me?
Maybe your foot.
Or maybe one of your hands."
"Ah, just how
am I going to give you one of my feet?"
"Then, better you give me . . .
better one of your eyes
you give to me.
You can see out of the other one!"
they say he said.
Then,
DGA: "Give it to me!" Wow!)

PSP: "Sta weno," xi.
Yak'an hab' b'at jun yol sat winh.

(DGA: Yol sat winh t'a . . .
PSP: Yo, masanto yak'b'at
jun yol sat winh.
Ixtota' yak'an hab' jun el.

Pero haxo t'a junel xo . . .
(DGA: Hi'.
PSP: Hatik ne'ik,
tas wal junh xo moo jun to (tik
tik) . . .
Yak'an hab' xi chimk'uhal
heb' winh.
"Hatik nek an.
ak' ts'in jab'ok xo t'ayin,
olin chamok."
"Tom ts'in hixtej pax wal jun si?"
Mejor ak' jun xoh
yol ha sat chi t'ayin," xi.
He, antonse yak'an hab' xi
b'at winh,
yo, skan haman winh b'i'an.
(DGA: Kan haman winh b'i'an.
PSP: Pero mok wa winh!
Ketkon hab' yek' winh,
ketkon yek' winh yonh . . .
(DGA: Ketkon yek' winh,
och wejel sk'ol winh jun,
PSP: Och wejel sk'ol winh chi',
kan haman winh.
A, tonse (tik tik) . . .
(DGA: Yak'an pensar winh.
PSP: "Ha chuman an,
ol hul hach wik'xi.
To tsin b'ati," xab' winh.

Sb'at winh chi' b'i'an.

PSP: "Okay," he said.
They say the man gave him one
of his eyes.
DGA: One of his eyes to . . .)
PSP: Yes, he even gave him
one of his eyes.
Thus they say he gave it to him the
first time.
But the next time . . .
DGA: Yes.)
PSP: Now,
what's the other way . . .

They say they got up the next morning.

"Now.
Give me a little something more,
I'm dying."
"Are you bothering me again?
"Better give another
of your eyes to me," he said.
Alright, and then he gave it to
him again,
yes, and he was left blind, then.
DGA: He was left blind, then.)
PSP: But he ate it!
The man staggered around,
he staggered around, and . . .
DGA: He staggered around,
his enemy was hungry.)
PSP: His enemy got hungry,
and he was left blind.
Ah, and then . . .
DGA: He started to think.)
PSP: "This is the way it'll be,
I'll come get you again.
I'm going, now," they say the man said.
[Closing]
And that man left, then.

Kan winh.

(DGA: B'at winh chi' b'i'an,

PSP: Tik ni hatob' k'itaxob' chi jun,
k'ochchi nok' ts'i' chi'.
Yo, (tik tik)...

"Tas wal to an. Ha'ach tik,
tas wala k'ulej," xab'.
"Machach?"
"Ha'in.
To an no ap
haxonhej ha k'inal wilnak."
(DGA: "Hak'nak pawor t'ayin," xi.

PSP: "Hak'nak ixim woch jun el.

A, hu'uj k'ochnak hin xi b'aj ayin.
Malaj pena.
Kotan t'a tik."
Haxob' nok' tsi' chi'
b'uyanb'at winh
(DGA: B'uyanb'at winh.
PSP: "Kotan te ask'ak'," xab' winh.
(DGA: He.
PSP: "Kotan t'ay yich jun te taj te'."

Ayab' jun k'ub'taj b'aj koch winh.

Yo, ayab' ek' winh ta'
sikb'anel jun,
sja hab' nok', nók' ch'akb'a chi'.
(DGA: Nok' ch'akb'a chi'.
PSP: Sk'ab' te'.
Haxob' yok'emta nok'.
(DGA: "Rauw!"
PSP: "Rauw!"
"To mas tsak hach willaj.
tsok toawia tsato wila'."

The man stayed behind.

DGA: That man left, then.)
[Background]
PSP: Not too much longer,
and that dog arrived.
Yes...
[Eighth (Peak) Event: Dialogue]
"What is this? You,
what are you doing?," they say he said.
"Who are you?"
"It's me.
It's just that
I just saw your condition."
DGA: "You're who did me a
favor," he said.)
PSP: "You're the one who gave me
maize to eat.
Ah, because of you I got back home.
Don't be afraid.
Come here."
And that dog led the man by the arm.

DGA: He led him by the arm.)
"Come, it's hot," they say he said.
DGA: Right.)
PSP: "Come over to the foot of this
pine tree."
They say there was a white pine where
they went.
Okay, they say when the man was
in the shade, then,
they say that hawk arrived.
DGA: That hawk.)
PSP: In a branch of the tree.
They say he was singing.
DGA: "Rauw!")
PSP: "Rauw!"
"I can't see you anymore.
I wish I could still see you."

(DGA: "Tsach wila'."

PSP: "Tope yuj chi',

tsach wilk'e'i

manhxalaj tas ayin.

Wan hin cham yuj wejel," xi.

"A, k'ehankot k'elan t'a tik,"

xab' nok' nok'.

(DGA: Ch'akb'a chi'.

PSP: Ch'akb'a chi' t'a winh.

"A, tom manxa jun ayuda

tsak' t'a chi',"

xab' nok' tz'i' chi' t'a winh

t'a nok' ch'akb'a chi'.

(DGA: T'a nok' ch'akb'a chi'.

PSP: Tonse (tik tik) . . .

"May, k'ehankot k'elan t'a tik,"

xab' nok' ch'akb'a chi'. "Yo."

(DGA: K'e k'elan winh.

PSP: Haxo ham nok'

xejkut yol sat winh,

haxob' t'a yol sat winh

em t'eb'najok, yo.

(DGA: Yos . . .

PSP: Yilan!

Yila'!

Yelixta k'enaj yol sat winh.

(DGA: Kanix sat winh chi' junel xo.

PSP: "Ak'kut jun xo," xab'i.

Yos, k'ex hab' k'elan jun yol jun.

B'at hab' xi jun xo yol sat winh chi'.

Yem hab' xi.

Yo, yochchi yol sat winh xchab'il.

(DGA: Yem junel xo.

PSP: Sb'oxi winh, b'i'an.

(DGA: B'oxi winh, b'i'an.

PSP: Ichnhejab' ta'.

Weno,

na'an ku'uj!

DGA: "I see you.")

PSP: "Perhaps because

I looked up to see you,

I don't have anything.

I'm going to die of hunger," he said.

"Ah, turn your head up here,"

they say the animal said.

DGA: The hawk.)

PSP: The hawk, to the man.

"Ah, he won't give you any help

from up there,"

they say the dog said to the man,

about that hawk.

DGA: About that hawk.)

PSP: Then . . .

"No, look up here!,"

they say the hawk said. "Right!"

DGA: The man looked up.)

PSP: And then the hawk

vomited up the man's eye,

and into the man's face, they say,

it came falling, right!

DGA: And . . .)

PSP: He could see!

He saw!

His sight came back again.

DGA: He had sight again!)

PSP: "Give me another one!"

And, he looked up again.

Another of his eyes came down again.

It fell also, they say.

So, the man's sight came back again.

DGA: Another one fell.)

PSP: The man was well again, then.

DGA: The man was well again, then.)

PSP: Just like that, they say.

[Closing]

Okay,

we remembered it!

CHAPTER 6

The Sorcerer

T HIS STORY, TOLD BY Francisco Santizo Andrés, was recorded in Huehuetenango on November 28, 1964, in the house Francisco and I rented
in the city of Huehuetenango. We had been working together since the
end of August, and he had recorded a number of brief texts, some biographical
and some procedural (agricultural work, salt extraction), some commentaries
on life in general (sickness and death). These texts had established our routine
of recording him in monologue, having him transcribe the tape and prepare a
rough Spanish translation, and me checking the transcription, extracting lexicon, and learning grammar. We met regularly to discuss what I was learning and
explore different domains of culture. Finally I asked him for a longer story, not a
personal experience, but a story people told to one another. This tale of a famous
warlock was the result.

This story is drawn from the native repertory, and it reports events believed
to have happened in the lives of living people. People and places are named, although the time frame is left undefined. The story concerns the evil deeds and ul-
timate destiny of a famous sorcerer, an *aj b'a'al*, a man who causes physical harm
to others through supernatural means, as opposed to the *aj k'o'ol*, who causes
spiritual harm. These two specialists form the class of *chuk winakil*, evil men.

People consist of three principal parts. The human body (*winak*) harbors the
soul. The soul is sometimes called *guapo* in local Spanish, *chiapah* in Chuj. It
resides in one's innards (*k'o'ol*, the contents of the body cavity, the center of the
emotions, like the European heart). The heart itself is *pixan*, a term that also
applies to a kind of spirit (Spanish *espíritu*) that comes to molest in the night,
feeling like a heavy weight on the chest that keeps one from breathing for several minutes.

K'o'ol is sometimes used in the sense of "soul." The soul is shared by the animal
counterpart (*snok'al k'o'ol*, the "animal of the soul"), an actual physical animal
that lives in this world and shares its fate with the human, including physical injury. These are real animals, but they are more than just animals. In the text that

follows, the narrator refers to them once as *heb' winh nok'*, "those [human-class] animals." One's personality comes from one's companion animal; some people are flighty as squirrels, but powerful men are believed to have pumas, coyotes, or even lightning and whirlwind as their animal counterparts (and truly powerful men may have more than one). The three elements interact in distinct spheres: humans with humans, souls with souls, animals with animals, but the results of their interaction in one sphere may resound in the other domains. Sorcerers work either through the spirit world, as *aj k'o'ol* (master of the soul) or through the physical world, as *aj b'a'al* (master of witchcraft). Or, they take on animal form and act on other such animals.

The Chuj community of San Mateo Ixtatán (*ko chonhab'*, "our selling place, our market, our village") is situated on the northern flanks of the Cuchumatán Mountains in the Department of Huehuetenango, Guatemala. Until recently, cloud forest covered the heights above the town (Breedlove and Hopkins 1970–71), and famous salt wells below the town gave it its name (from Nahuat "place of salt"). The town of San Mateo is divided into several neighborhoods (Spanish *cantón*, loaned to Chuj as *kantonh*). Outside the bounds of the town itself are subsidiary settlements (Spanish *aldea*, Chuj *k'alu'um*, literally, "old land"). These in turn have smaller dependencies (Spanish *caserío*). The events reported in this story took place in and around Yolaquitac (*yola' kitak* "Kitak river," meaning unknown), a caserío of the aldea Jolomtenam (*jolom tenam*, "head of the rock outcrop"), one of the five major aldeas of San Mateo. Every subdivision of the community—cantones, aldeas, caseríos—is said to have its own sorcerers, and these men are powerful politically and socially as well as being sorcerers. The three that are named in this story are Tunku Matal, a good man; Xan Malin, an evil man, both residents of Yolaquitac; and Maltix Ros, the chief sorcerer for all of San Mateo. These names are the equivalent of Spanish Domingo Magdalena, Juan María, and Baltazar Rosa (or perhaps Rosario). Curiously, all three combine male and female names, not the usual patronymic and first name of the father, as the narrator, Francisco Santizo Andrés, is the son of Andrés Santizo [Antonio].

Sorcerers take some of their powers from objects; in this story, Xan Malin carries a medallion (*medaya*, a loan from Spanish) that confers on him multiple "souls," referred to as *smoj animah*, yet another term for the *chiapah*, combining *moj* "afterbirth" with *animah* "person," literally "the person's afterbirth." These multiple souls allowed him to be able to take any form he chose, examples being a leaf, a woman, an animal, or just anything. He also carried a metal cane and a knife, referred to as "his two companions" (*chab' yet'b'eyum*, "two that accompany him on his walks"). The medallion survived the sorcerer's death, and its later conduct suggests that it may have been a motivating factor in his philandering, urging him to go out to drink and molest women.

After the necessary background, the narrator gives a detailed account of Xan Malin's evil deeds. He goes out at night to enter houses, molest the women of the household and eat their food. He follows girls that attract his attention and goes into their houses at night. He does all this without being detected, even sleeping with women at the sides of their husbands. However, when drunk he brags about his deeds, and the community becomes aware of his acts. The other sorcerers confer and decide to attack him with sorcery (as *aj b'a'al*). But they could not cause physical harm to him because he was too powerful. Next they sent out their companion animals (*snok'al sk'o'ol*), with no better result. Finally, they lure him to a meeting by pretending to be the chief sorcerer, Maltix Ros, and give him bewitched alcohol to drink. When he is thoroughly drunk, they fall on him (his physical body, *winak*) and beat him, chop him with a machete, and hit him with clubs, but he fights back and wounds several of them. Then they stab him with a knife, and his spirit (*sk'o'ol*) departs his body.

The men are able to carry his body to a cliff and throw it off; body parts are strewn down the side of the rock face. But when they reach the bottom to check on their work, he is getting up. They beat him again, even gutting him and tearing out his heart, but his foot is still capable of kicking them. He is beat again until his testicles come off. Then they leave his remains there. A day later they return to hide his body, but he is too heavy to lift. Their animals are summoned, and pumas take turns carrying the weight to a wilderness named Catelac (*k'atelak*, named after a wildflower, *k'ate'*). Coyotes arrive to eat his flesh.

His wife is not worried about his disappearance, since he is accustomed to leave for days on end. But while she is asleep he begins to arrive at night and work spinning and weaving wool (a man's job). When his son goes out to check on the family cornfield, Xan Malin speaks to him and says he is staying out there to watch the corn. Then one day a finger appears on the wife's blanket. She takes this as a sign he is dead, and alerts the authorities. When his remains are discovered, there are only bones and his head, with a scarf and his wool jacket (Spanish *capixay*, Chuj *lopil*). Even after all is taken away, one of his spirits (*jun spixan*) remains, and he appears to people walking by, greeting them and chatting them up.

The authorities draw up a report of his death, and one of them finds the medallion and takes it home. At night it speaks to him, urging him to get up and go out and have some fun! He can't sleep through it, and he throws the medallion away. Many men were arrested and jailed for the killing of Xan Malin, but they spent little time in jail, since no evidence could be brought to bear on the question of who was responsible for the death.

The narrator now goes back and reviews some of the powers of Xan Malin and relates that at the time of his death, black buzzards and red-headed vultures (*hostok* and *xulem*) arrived to fight with the men, along with many other animals and a whirlwind (*chak xuxum ik'*), tossing the men around. Finally, a large rock, another of his *smoj animah*, came crashing through the group, striking them, and then a great fire and a lot of other things. But he died. There were many witnesses to these acts.

The Sorcerer

Narrator: Francisco Santizo Andrés, of San Mateo Ixtatán, Huehuetenango, Guatemala

Recorded in Huehuetenango, November 28, 1964

Chuj Text 12 [CAC 002 R012]

[Opening]

Antonse swik'ti'ej winh anima chi',
porke tob' te aj b'al winh.
Yuj chi', ha syalan anima,
tob' hanhej wal winh te chuk.
Yuj chi', masanil anima ts'alani,
aykan yik'ti'al winh.
Porke (te sobre te') mas te aj b'al winh,
t'a yichanh jantak masanil heb' winh
aj b'al t'a yol chonhab'.
Ay heb' winh yichamtak winakil
aj b'al t'ay yol chonhab'.
Porke ha smodo heb' winh ta',
t'ay jun jun kantonh,
ay jun jun heb' winh ichamtak wínak
sat aj b'a'al.
Ha heb' winh sb'ohan
yaj t'a yol chonhab'.
Ay jun jun heb' winh pax
t'ay jun jun k'alu'um.
Yuj chi', tato ay junh lolonel
sb'o heb' winh, ts'el ab'is
t'ay masanil jantak heb' winh
ayel t'ay jun jun k'alu'um.
Smolchaj heb' winh,
syalan junh slolonel heb' winh.

Yuj chi', t'ay jun k'alum chi',
t'ay yola kitak, ha ta'
ay jun winh skuchan Tunhku Matal.
Ha winh skuchan Tunhku Matal chi',

So, I will talk about a man
who was a great sorcerer.
So, people say
only he was very powerfully evil.
So, everyone talks about him;
there is an enduring story about him.
Because he was the greatest sorcerer
among all those other men who are
sorcerers in San Mateo Ixtatán.
There are many elder men who are
sorcerers in the village center.
Because the manner of those men is,
in each cantón,
each has its elder men,
the head men of sorcery.
Those men arrange things
that go on in the village center.
There are also those men
in each aldea.
So, if there is a meeting
those men make, the notice goes out
to all the other men
who are out in each aldea.
They gather, those men,
and they have a discussion.

[Xan Malin's evil deeds]

So, in one aldea there,
in Yolaquitac, there
there is a man named Tunku Matal.
That man named Tunku Matal,

hab' winh tik te aj b'al ta' yalani.
Pero ay junxo winh,
skuchan Xan Malin.
Yuj chi', ha heb' winh cha wanh chi',
ha heb' winh sat aj b'al
yaj t'a yol k'alum chi'.
Pero ha winhaj Tunhku Matal chi',
ha wach'il syak' winh,
malaj puch winakil syak' winh chi'.
Wen omre syutej sb'a winh.
Pero haxo winhaj Xan Malin chi jun,
komo mas te chukab' winh.
Yuj chi', ts'ek' wal winh
yib'anh hab' xchukal.
Pero manhoklaj wach'il chi'
syak' winh,
ha puch winakil syak' winh.
Ix yilelta winh,
ke syempre mas te chuk winh,
t'a yichanh masanil heb' winh aj b'al
t'ay chonhab',
t'ay jun jun k'alu'um.
Entonse, haxo winh puch winakil
ix yak'k'e winh.
Yos, ayab' jun k'en smedaya winh, xi.
Yuj chi',
ha hab' k'en smedaya winh chi' yet'i,
itob' te tsijtum smoj yanima winh.
Yuj chi', hab' yilelta winh,
ke to max wal tsak'wanlaj
masanil heb' winh syal sb'a
aj b'alil chi' t'a winh.
Entonse ix b'at winh t'ay jun
jun k'alu'um,
t'a masanil yol chonhab',
ts'och winh pojoj pat.
Ix yilelta winh jun,
malaj tas syak' pasar t'a winh,

they say he was a great sorcerer.
But there is another man,
named Xan Malín.
So, those two men,
they were the chief sorcerers
there in the center of the aldea.
But that gentleman Tunku Matal,
he did good,
he wasn't a trouble-maker.
He acted as a good man.
But that other gentleman Xan Malín,
was more evil, they say.
So, he succeeded
through his evil, they say.
But it wasn't good that he did,

he made himself a trouble-maker.
He saw
that he was certainly more powerful
than all of the other sorcerers
in the village,
and in each aldea.
So, that evil man
made trouble for them.
Well, they say he had a medallion.
So, they say,
that medallion he had with him
gave him many companion spirits.
So, they say he saw
that they could not match him,
all those who called themselves
sorcerers.
So he went to each aldea,

in the whole village,
and he broke into the houses.
He saw, then,
nothing would happen to him,

max ilchaj'eltalaj wính.
I hasta heb' winh te aj b'al chi yalani,
ts'och winh t'a yol spat heb' winh.
I ha b'at k'ulok winh t'a yol spat chi',
ts'och winh t'a yol te pat,
porke toton puch winak winh.
(ix och) Ix yilelta winh,
te wach' yaj yoch winh yol te pat.
Malaj mach tas ts'alani,
i malaj mach tsak'wan t'a winh.
Entonse ha xo heb' ix ix,
haxob' heb' ix, b'at yixtej winh.
Tsab' yil winh mach heb' ix anima
te wach' yilji.
Tonhej syilkan heb' ix winh
t'a jun k'u,
ha xo t'ay t'ak'walil, sb'at winh.
Sk'och winh t'a te pat chi',
yos, b'at pojan'och sb'a winh.
Komo te chuk winh jun,
tsab' ochk'och winh yol pat chi'.
Tsab' yak'ankan'em ts'ikan
jun kantela winh,
ts'em wokan winh, swa winh.
Tato ay hab' ixim wa'il,
tato ay tas swach' wa'el,
uk'el aykani, tsab' say yil winh.
Ana' anima,
waynak t'a yol spat.
Ts'och sk'ak' winh,
swa winh, kontento.
Slajwi hab' swa winh,
ayuch ts'ikan jun kantela chi'
yil yok winh.
Despwes, sk'och winh
t'ay b'ajtil sway ix
yet' winh yichmil.
Pero ha winh chi jun,

he would not be discovered.
And even to those great sorcerers
he entered into their houses.
And what he went to do there,
he would enter into the house,
because he was a trouble-maker.
He saw
how easy it was to enter the house.
Nobody said anything,
and nobody was his equal.
So, the women,
those women, he would molest them.
He would see which of the women
were best looking.
He would just see them one day,

and then at night, he would go.
He entered into the house,
well, he broke into the house.
Since he was really powerful,
they say he would enter the house.
They say he would leave lit
a candle,
he would sit down, and eat.
If there were any tortillas, they say,
if there was anything good to eat
or to drink left, he would look for it.
And those people,
asleep in their house.
He would make a fire,
he would eat, content.
He would finish eating, they say,
and leave a candle burning
so he could see.
Later, he would arrive
at where the woman was sleeping
with her husband.
But that man,

machekel tas xom syutej
heb' winh anima chi winh.
Tsab' te ochkan swayanh
heb' winh yichmil heb' ix chi'.
Yuj chi', mab'ax yab'laj heb' winh,
sk'och winh.
Snitschajkan'el heb' winh,
t'ay sts'ey heb' ix,
sway winh yet' heb' ix winh.
Kontento, syixtan heb' ix winh.

———

who knows what he did
to those people.
They say they would stay asleep,
those husbands of the women.
So, they didn't hear anything
when he arrived.
They would be moved away
from the side of the women;
he slept with the women.
Content, he molested the women.

———

I hanheja hab' syutej sb'a winh chi',
wach' chomab' ha jun ix kob'es.
Tato, toxo ix kanab' snab'en
winh, t'ay ix,
toxo ix yil ix winh ke tato
wach' yilji ix,
ha xo t'a t'ak'walil sk'och winh,
b'at yixtan ix winh, b'at way
winh yet' ix.
Ix ek' nhej mul, yak'an winh ichachi'.
Despwes, ix yilan winh jun,
malaj mach tas ts'alani.
Max spaklaj sb'a heb' winh
anima chi',
hasta max yileltalaj heb' winh
tato ay mach tik ts'ixtan
yajal yistsil heb' winh t'ay sts'ey.

———

And just so, they say he would do,
if he saw an unmarried girl.
If he were attracted to her,

if he saw she was good looking,

then at night he would arrive,
go molest her, go sleep with her.

He just sinned like this.
Later, he saw, then,
nobody said anything.
The men didn't defend themselves,

they didn't even see
if there was someone toying with
their wives at their sides.

———

Pero haxo winh jun,
komo toton te chuk winh
sna'ani,
malaj mach stsak'wani.
Haxo winh ts'alan'elta t'a sti'.
Haxo winh ts'alani, ke
"Ha'in tik, jantak masanil heb' winh
ay t'ay chonhab' tik,
jantak heb' winh wet ajk'alumal tik,

But that man,
since he was so powerful
he thought to himself,
there was nobody who equaled him.
He began to talk.
That man would say that:
"As for me, all of those men
that are in the village,
so many of our aldea neighbors,

wan xo wek'chaj t'ay spatik
yajal yistsil heb' winh, smasanil.
Wojtak xo chajtil yaj yistsil heb' winh.
May ts'och heb' winh,
may jab'ok swach'il heb' winh,
may icha unin,
ichachi' yaj heb' winh t'ayin.
Ina heb' winh syal sb'a
yajal chonhab'il
t'a yol jun jun k'alu'um,
te chuk heb' winh yalani,
pero ha heb' winh chi',
b'ab'el ix wak' prowal
heb' ix yajal yistsil,
yal yisil heb' winh.
Te noy, te wach'.
Wik yaji.
(may) May winh mach tas ts'alani,
ha'in swala'.
I pax heb' winh ay t'a yol chonhab',
heb' winh yajal chonhab',
heb' winh yichamtak winakil,
yal yisil heb' winh,
yajal yistsil heb' winh,
syempre wak' prowar.
Wan xo hin nanh pojax ek'
t'ay yol chonhab' tik.
Hin sayan wil yajal yistsil
heb' winh chonhab' tik
t'a yol chonhab',"
xchab' winh, ichatik.

I am getting on the backs
of their wives, all of them.
I know how they are, their wives.
They are worthless, those men,
they are no good, those men,
they are like children,
that's how they are to me.
Those men who call themselves
the lords of the village
in every aldea,
very powerful men, they say,
but those men,
I first tried out
the women that are their wives,
the daughters of those men.
Very nice. Very good.
They are mine.
Nobody says anything,
I say.
And also those men in San Mateo,
those lords of the town,
those elder men,
the daughters of those men,
the wives of those men,
I certainly have tried them.
Already I am half way
through the village.
I look for the wives
of the men of the village
in the center of the town,"
said the man, thus.

———

Syalan winh, syuk'an anh anh winh,
jantak sk'ak'b'ik'och winh
yuj anh anh,
yos, syalan'elta winh.
Porke syil winh jun,
ke to malaj mach

He talked, when he was drinking,
he got so heated up with alcohol,

well, he would speak out.
Because he saw
that there was nobody who

sts'ak'wan t'a winh.

Entonse, hanheja' chi',
ix yab'an heb' winh
jantak heb' winh chuk chi jun,
ke to ichachi' syal winh.
Entonse ix sayan yil heb' winh, b'i'an.
Ix smaklan heb' winh,
ke ta to yel syal winh,
to syak' puch winakil winh.
Pero ix yilelta heb' winh jun,
to yel syal winh.
Sk'och nhej winh t'a te pat chi',
t'ay jantak t'ay skyere,
i mach ix anima chi'
b'aj skan snab'en winh,
b'at way nhej winh yet' ix.

——

Yuj chi', k'ojanh k'olal,
ix yak' wenta heb' winh,
jantak masanil aj b'al chi',
ke to hanhej wal winh ts'akan jun chi'
t'ay sch'okojil.
Yos, ix sayan heb' winh
chajtil modo satel winh.
Porke masanil nanam kistal,
masanil jantak heb' winh chonhab',
ha heb' winh chi',
chuk syab'i ke to ha heb' ix
yajal yistsil heb' winh, syixtej winh.
I mismu t'a sts'ey heb' winh tik,
sway winh yet' heb' ix.

Yuj chi', ha smul winh chi',
k'ojanh k'olal,
ix te molchaj smul winh
t'ay heb' winh jantak masaníl.
Ix saychaj b'i'an,

could equal him.
[People take notice]
So, just like that,
they heard,
so many of the powerful men,
that he talked like this.
So they tried to see, then.
They watched to see
if it was true what he said,
if he was a trouble-maker.
But they saw,
what he said was true.
He just arrived at a house,
as many as he wanted,
and whatever woman
that he wanted,
he just went and slept with her.

So, slowly,
they realized,
all those sorcerers,
that he alone was making trouble
for the others.
Well, they looked
for a way to lose him.
Because all the tame dumb ones,
all the many people of the village,
those people,
took it badly that the women
that were their wives, he molested.
And right there at their sides,
he slept with them.
[Sorcery fails]
So, his misbehavior, slowly,

his misbehavior built up
against all those men.
They looked for something, then,

tas ix ik'an xcham winh.
Pero komo malaj winh
ts'och sk'ab' t'a winh,

malaj winh (winh) sk'ochwal b'at
mak'an winh,
malaj winh tas ol utan wal winh.
I hasta ix yak'laj hab' heb' winh,
primero t'ay b'a'al.
Ijan ix sb'alej winh heb' winh,
pero komo te chuk winh,
mas ts'ek' winh
t'a yib'anh heb' winh.
Entonse,
lwego syil hab' heb' winh, xi,
ay manh syilelta winh,
ke to ay jun winh aj b'a'al,
entonse syaman winh heb' winh, yos,
una wes (smak') smak'ab' heb'
winh winh.
Yuj chi',
xiw heb' winh jantak anima
chi' t'a winh.

that would bring about his death.
But there was nobody
who would put his hand
against him,
there was nobody to come
beat up on him,
nobody to do anything to him.
And the men even tried, they say,
first with sorcery.
When they worked sorcery on him,
since he was very powerful,
all the more he came out
on top of them.
So,
right away the men saw, they say,
as soon as the man saw
that it was a sorcerer,
then he grabbed them, and
once and for all he beat them.

So,
many people were afraid of him.

———

Ay jun makanh xo heb' winh –
nok', xi.
Komo hanhej wala' yek' winh chi'.
Wach' chom masanil hab' t'ay
t'ak'walil,
skot winh t'a b'aj ay,
skot winh t'ay kal chonhab'.
Snak'e winh
b'ajtil ol k'och winh t'a junh ak'wal,
t'a junh k'alu'um.
Jantak chiman ak'wal,
sb'at winh, sk'och winh,
t'a junh k'alu'um.

[Attack in the jungle]
There is another part of men—
an animal, they say.
So just like that he would go out.
Even in the dead of night,

he would go wherever,
he would go through the town.
He would decide
where all he would go that night,
to an aldea.
Along about midnight,
he would go out, arrive
at some aldea.

Hanheja' jun chukal chi' b'at
yak' winh.
Ayab' jun k'en sk'okoch k'en winh,
yet' jun skuchilub' winh.
Ha hab' wal
chab' yetb'eyum winh chi'.
Yuj chi', tsab' snak'e winh,
sb'at winh jantak t'ak'walil.
Sb'at nhej winh t'a yok,
i malaj syak' pasar t'a winh.
Wach' chom ay winh aj k'olab'
smak'am winh t'a yol b'e,
may ts'och heb' winh.
May malaj jab'ok b'aj
ts'och heb' winh yuj winh,
porke mas ts'ek' winh
yib'anh heb' winh.
Despwes, ix yilan winh
ke to malaj ts'och heb' winh chi',
yo, mas nhej ste'ak'ej puch
winakil winh,
mas nhej te kot yowal winh
yak'an stsuntsan heb' ix ix.

——

Pero ha heb' winh masanil chi jun,
komo toxo ix och t'ay xchikin
heb' winh,
toxo ix yaweb' [yab' heb'] winh,
chajtil to hajun chi syak' winh,
entonse ix te molchaj smul winh.
Hab' yak'lan heb' winh masanil chi'
t'ay b'a'al chi'.
Maj yallaj yuj heb' winh.
Haxob' "T'a heb' winh nok',"
ix yal heb' winh,
"mejor cht'on ts'ek' winh t'ay
t'ak'walil,
mejor smak'chaj winh t'a yol b'e,

Like that, to do evil he would go out.

They say he had a metal cane,
and a knife.
Those were
his two companions, they say.
So, when he would decide to
he would go out many nights.
He would just go out on foot,
and nothing would happen to him.
Even if an enemy, they say,
attacked him on the road,
they couldn't do anything.
there was no place where
they could get the better of him,
because he always came out
on top of them.
Later, he saw
that they couldn't deal with him,
and he just went on making trouble,

he just got worse
at molesting the women

But all of those men,
since it already entered their ears,

they already had heard it,
how he was behaving,
and his evil deeds were piled up.
They say all those men tried
sorcery.
it didn't work on him.
So they say, "With the animals,"
said those men,
"better, as he goes out at night,

better he be attacked on the road

i una wes hata'
slajwel winh,"
xchab' heb' winh.
Ha xo heb' winh
ay snok'al sk'o'ol,
nok' chój, nok' (tas) okes,
(nok') tastak nok'al,
tsab' makan winh
t'a yol b'e.
Komo ay jun yaxlum
t'ay yib'anhk'eta
t'a b'aj ay sk'alum winh chi',
hata' skot sb'e winh,
sja' t'ay chonhab'.

Yuj chi', jantak ora
snak'e winh skoti,
skot nhej winh t'a t'ak'walil,
sja winh t'a chonhab'.
I masanil tyempo,
uk'uma'anh [uk'um anh anh] winh.

Yuj chi',
t'a jun nanhal yaxlum chi',
ha hab' ta' smak'chaj winh
yuj nok' choj chi'.
Ay jun lot'il tenam,
ha hab' ta' smak'chaj winh.
Pero tsab' k'ehul winh ta',
ayek' nok' choj chi',
tsab' yalan winh,
"Elanhek t'a yol hin b'e.
Elanhek t'a yol hin b'e,
porke manhokexlaj
tsek'ex hin say wila'.
Ha'in tik,
to tsin b'eyek' t'ay yol wiko',

and there, once and for all
he'll be finished,"
they say those men said.
Then all those men
who had spirit animals,
lion, coyote,
whatever animal,
they say they attacked him
on the road.
Since there is a jungle
up above
where his aldea was,
there his path went
when he came to town.

So, whenever
he thought to get up,
he would get up in the night,
he would come to town.
And all the time,
he would be drunk.

So,
in the middle of the jungle there,
there, they say, he was attacked
by those pumas.
There is a narrow pass in the rock,
they say there he was attacked.
But when he got there, they say,
those pumas were there;
they say he said,
"Get out of my road.
Get out of the middle of my road,
because it's not you all
I'm out looking for.
As for me,
I'm passing through my own
territory,

ini hex tik ne'ik,
syempre
ay b'aj tsex b'eyek'i.
Tsena' b'eyek' he b'a,
ichachi waji.
Malaj mach tsex makani,
malaj mach tas ts'alan t'ayex.
Ichachi' waji.
Ay hin derechu hin b'eyek'i,"
xchab' winh ichatik
t'a nok' choj chi'.
Pero ha nok' jun,
tonhej hab' stsewaj nok',
max ellaj nok'
t'a yol sb'e winh.
Komo nok' nok' jun
tekan xiw winh
t'ay nok' sna'ani.
Pero ha xo winh jun,
mab'ax xiwlaj winh.
Tsab' yalan winh,
"Tato maxex el t'a yol hin b'e
t'a ak'an k'olal,
entonse (olin) yala' tas
olin aj heyet'ok,"
xchab' winh ichatik.
Pero jantak syal hab' winh
t'ay nok',
max ellaj nok'.
Jun xo, stsaktsajk'e winh,
skot yowal winh, yos,
tsab' och yub'naj winh
t'ay sjaj nok',
tsab' syumanh nok' winh,
syumanhkanb'at nok' winh
t'ay kaltak yaxlu'um. (Skot winh
t'ay . . .)
Skot winh

and you all,
certainly
there is a place for you all to walk.
Think about walking,
that's the way I am.
Nobody is attacking you,
nobody is saying anything to you.
That's the way I am.
I have the right to walk around,"
they say the man spoke thus
to those pumas.
But those animals,
they say they just laughed,
the animals didn't leave
the middle of the road.
Since those animals, well,
maybe he was afraid
of the animals, they thought.
But that man, well,
he wasn't afraid.
They say he said,
"If you all don't get out of my path
of your own accord,
then there is something
I will do to you,"
they say the man spoke thus.
But for all that he said, they say,
to the animals,
they didn't leave.
So, he got tired of this,
he got angry, then,
they say he grabbed one
by the animal's throat,
they say he threw the animal,
he threw the animals off
into the jungle.

He stayed there

t'ay yol b'e chi b'i'an.
Syak'an segir winh sb'eyi.
Yuj chi',
ix yilan'elta heb' winh chi jun,
ke te malaj ts'och heb' winh,
max tsak'wanlaj heb' winh (t'ay)
t'ay winh.

Yos,
"Tas wal modo ol ik'an xcham winh,
porke sko mak winh,
i ijan sko b'alej winh,
pero (max) max yallaj,
max techajlaj winh ku'uj.
Mas te chuk winh,"
xchab' heb' winh ichatik.
Pero ix te' ak'an wal pensar heb' winh
tas modoal ol cham winh.
"Bweno,
entonse ha xo t'ay jun tyempo," xi,
"ham k'och ijan pax swerte winh."
Yos,
t'a jun Pasku halab' junel, xi,
komo tom chekel jantak heb' winh,
yamigu pax winh jun,
komo ha ta' t'a hantes chi',
masanil heb' winh anima,
heb' winh chonhab',
xiw heb' winh
t'a heb' winh aj b'a'al.
Tos yak'uch . . .
[tape ends; new tape begins]
Yuj chi',
tsab' xiw heb' winh
t'ay masanil heb' winh aj b'a'al.
Yuj chi',
to syak'uch sb'a heb' winh
t'ay heb' winh.

in the middle of the road, then.
He went on with his walk.
So,
those men saw
that they couldn't handle him,
they couldn't bother him.

[A new plan emerges]
So,
"How can we make him die,
because we attack him,
and we use sorcery on him,
but it isn't possible,
we can't defeat him.
He is more powerful,"
they say the men spoke thus.
But they really thought about
how he would die.
"Okay,
then sometime," they said,
"his destiny ought to arrive."
So,
one Christmas Eve, they say,
since many people were called,
even that man's friends,
since for a long time
all the people,
the people of the town,
were afraid
of those sorcerers.
So . . .

So,
they say they were afraid
of all those sorcerers.
So,
they joined with
those men.

Te' yikab'il heb' winh aj b'al chi'
yuj heb' winh.
Yuj chi',
malaj mach stsuntsan winh
t'ay ak'an k'olal,
malaj mach tas ts'alan t'a winh.
Pero ha xo heb' winh masanil chi jun,
ix yak'an'el lolonel heb' winh.
Masanil heb' winh jantak kotak unin,
masanil ichamtak winak ix tak'wi,
masanil heb' winh chonhab'.
Ix tak'wi t'a spatik winh,
ke to syal xcham winh.
"Porke ini honh tik, kotak unin honh.
B'ak'inh ol k'e ko k'ib'i,
repenta ol ko say ix kajal kistsil,
repenta toxo ix ek' winh
t'ay spatik heb' ix,
ol lik'an heb' íx.
E mato ol kik' ko b'a yet' heb' ix,
ha xo winh, ol b'at ixtan
heb' ix t'ayonh,
porke to ha jun chi syak' winh,"
xchab' heb' winh masanil.
Ix tak'wi heb' winh
t'a spatik winh to xcham winh.

Yuj chi',
ix k'ochab' yempu t'ay Pasku chi',
ix smolan sb'a heb' winh b'i'an.
Ayamab' junh trenta homre, xi.

Heb' winh aj b'al chi wal,
ix och sk'ab' chi' t'ay winh.
Komo ayab' jun te pat
b'ajtil wal uk'wi'anh winh jun,
winh aj b'al chi'.
I ch'okab' junxo te pat

Very respected were sorcerers
by those men.
So,
nobody bothered him
voluntarily,
nobody said anything to him.
But all of the people
called a meeting.
All the many children,
all the elders answered,
all the villagers.
They met behind his back,
to see if his death was possible.
"Because we, we are the children.
When we grow up,
then we will find wives,
then he will go out
on the backs of the women,
he will molest the women.
And if we marry the women,
that man, he'll go toy with
the women on us,
because that's what he does,"
they say they all said.
The people responded
behind his back, that he should die.
[The plan is executed]
So,
they say that Christmas came,
the men gathered, then.
There were about thirty
men, they say.
The sorcerers were there,
who put their hands against him.
Since there was a house
where that man would drink,
that sorcerer.
And apart, they say, another house

t'a b'ajtil ix smolb'ej sb'a heb' winh,
heb' winh skontra winh chi'.
Yuj chi',
"Mejor tas wal skutej scham
winh tik ne'ik
ko b'o'ek,
hanhej wal ijan slajwel winh t'ay
t'a ak'wal tik,"
xchab' heb' winh.
Hab' smanan anh anh heb' winh,
hab' yuk'an anh heb' winh.
Pero ha heb' winh,
heb' winh ayuch snab'en
smak'ancham winh chi',
mab'ax yuk'laj anh heb' winh.
Ayab' jun woteya
anh anh chi'
ch'ok ix yik'el heb' winh.
Hab' sb'alej anh heb' winh,
xchi.
Porke ichachi' syutej heb'
winh yalani,
hab' sb'alej anh heb' winh.
Tas xomab' ix yutej anh heb'
winh, yos,
ch'okab' ix yik'el anh heb' winh.
Yik wal winh.
Tato ol k'och winh t'a skal heb'
winh chi',
yos,
ha hab' anh chi' ol yak' winh.
Yuk' winh,
yik ol el yip winh, yos,
hab' mak'ancham winh heb' winh.
Hab' b'okan'el chi jun,
ix yak' lista heb' winh masanil, yos,
ayab' winh xchekab' heb' winh,
ix b'ati.

where the men gathered,
the men who were his enemies.
So,
"Better what we do to kill him now

we do it,
however we resolve to finish him
tonight,"
they say the men said.
They say they bought alcohol,
they say they were drinking.
But those men,
those men who wanted
to beat him to death,
they didn't drink.
They say there was a bottle
of alcohol
they set aside.
They say they bewitched the alcohol,
they say.
Because thus they did, they say,

they say they bewitched the alcohol.
Who knows what they did to it, but

they set the alcohol aside, they say.
It was his.
When he arrived among them,

well,
that alcohol they would give to him.
He would drink it,
he would lose his strength, and
they would beat him to death.
When that was prepared, well,
they all got ready, and,
they say they had a messenger,
he went out.

Xit' chekankot winh t'ay b'ajay
ayek' chi'.
Hab' t'a sb'ab'elal,
ix yal hab' winh chi',
"To tsach b'ati.
To ayek' heb' winh ichamtak winak
hach stanhwej t'ay tik,"
xchab' winh t'ay (heb') winh.
Pero ha xo winh jun,
maj kotlaj winh.
Pero hab' winh,
wanab' yuk'an anh winh.
I syempre ha winh chi',
komo tob' te' toton hab' te chuk winh,
i syalab' yoch winh (masanil)
masanil forma, xi.
Yuj chi',
pero yuj anh anh chi',
maj xo yal sb'ohan'och sb'a winh,
maj so yalam sayan yil winh.
Yuj chi',
hab' t'a xcha'el t'a yox'el, yos,

haxob' ix k'ochix winh chekab' chi'
junel xo,
hab' yalan winh t'ay winh,
"To tik ha winhaj icham
Maltix Ros," xi.
Porke ha winhaj Maltix Ros chi',
t'a yol chonhab' ay winh,
i sat aj b'al winh
t'ay yol chonhab'.
Yuj chi',
haxob' winh
ix yesej'el sti'ok heb' winh molan chi'

ke to ha winh ix k'och t'a skal
hab' winh.

He went out to summon him.

They say the first time,
they say he said to him,
"Come.
There are Elders
waiting for you now,"
they say he said to him (them).
But that man, well,
he didn't come.
But they say that he
was drinking.
And certainly that man,
since he was so powerful,
and he could take on
all forms, they say.
So,
but because of the alcohol,
he couldn't do it,
he couldn't manage to do it.
So,
they say the second or third
time, well,
they say that messenger arrived
once again;
they say he said to him,
"That elder gentleman Maltix
Ros," he said.
Because that gentleman Maltix Ros
he was from the town center,
and he was the chief sorcerer
in San Mateo.
So,
that man,
the men who were gathered
lied about him
so that that man would
come to them.

Yuj chi',

"Tsach b'ati," xchi winh chekab' chi',

"Ix k'och winh t'a winh."

Yuj chi',

"Ma'ay. Tato ha winh ix jawi jun,

mejor totonam olin b'atok.

Ol b'at wab'i tas yal winh

tato ix jawi winh,"

xchab' winh (t'ay) t'a winh

chekab' chi'.

Ixtota' skotab' winh b'i'an.

Sk'ochab' winh t'a te pat,

t'a b'ajtil molan heb' winh chi jun.

"B'aj a(y) winh icham chi',

aj a(y) winh icham Maltix chi',"

xchab' winh ichatik, sk'och winh.

"Tik ochanhkoti,

malaj winh,

ha'onh ton tik, xit'ach ko

chek ik'naxok,

komo ina max wal honh a k'anab'ajej.

Yuj chi', ha winh ix kesej'el sti'ok,

tsach jawi.

To t'a ko gana,

t'a ko nab'en skak' junh a trago,

skuk' junh anh t'a ak'an k'olal

yak b'a ayach'ek'pax kat'

t'a yol ko k'alum jun.

Porke ha'ach tik,

ay b'aj t'ay ch'ok k'alumal,

t'a yol chonhab'

ay b'aj ha ta' tsach b'ati.

Hok xo yakb'a ayach'ek'

t'a yol ko k'alu'um,

kuk' junh ko trago,

t'ay wach',

t'ay ak'an k'olal.

Yuj chi', xit'ach ko chek ik'naxok,

So,

"Come," said the messenger,

"He came to them."

So,

"Well. If that man has come, then,

maybe it's better if I go.

I'll go to hear what he says

if he has come,"

they say he said to the messenger.

So they say he came, then.

They say he arrived at that house

where the men were gathered.

"Where is that Elder?

Where is that Elder Maltix?,"

so said the man, when he arrived.

"Come in here,

he's not here,

it was us, we sent our messenger

to get you,

since you wouldn't respond to us.

So, that man spoke falsely,

so you would come.

It's our desire,

that we thought to give you a drink,

to drink some alcohol if you will

now that you're here with us

in the middle of our aldea.

Because you,

there are times that to other aldeas,

to the village center,

there are times you go there.

Now that you're here

in the middle of our aldea,

let's have a drink,

for the good,

voluntarily.

So, we sent our messenger to bring you,

pero ini, pural ixach koti.

Yuj chi', ha to winh icham chi'
ix kesej'el sti'ok,
yos tsach jawi.
Pero malaj tas kal t'ayach an,

to hanhej jun kanh skuk'ej.
Slajwi.
Malaj tas'i yik jun nhej tsonh aji,"
xchab' heb' winh t'a winh.
"Tato ichachi',
syal kuk'ani."
"Tom ay syal jun,
toton k'inh ayonh,"
xchab' winh.
"Entonse huk' junh a trago an,"
xchaweb' winh t'ay winh, yos.
Pero ch'ok yaj anh yik winh
(ix) ix sb'alaj hab' heb' winh chi'.
Haxob' anh yak' heb' winh
yuk' winh,
te chamk'och hab' winh yuj
anh jun, yos.
Tik yalan hab' heb' winh b'i'an, yos,
"Una wes skak'ej t'a winh,
porke xal ta ma'ay, (olonh)
wan yek' ak'wal.
Olonh sakb'ok'ochi, yos,
ke tal manh ol cham winh ku'uj,"
schab' heb' winh.

Entonse ay wal winh mas wiwu
chi', (ix)
ix koti, yos,
ix b'ab'laj mak'an winh.
Ix k'e b'uynaj heb' winh b'i'an,
ix sayan'elta howal chi heb' winh.

but look, it was hard to
make you come.
So, those elders
they spoke falsely,
so you would come.
But we don't have anything to
say to you,
we are just having a drink.
That's all.
There's no reason we're here,"
they say they said to him.
"If that's the way it is,
it's possible we can drink."
"If it's possible, then,
we're just having a party,"
they say the men said.
"Then have a drink,"
they say the men said to him, then.
But set aside was the drink for him
that they had bewitched, they say.
So they gave him that drink to drink,

and he got very drunk with it, then.

Now they say they said, then,
"Once and for all let's give it to him,
because if not, (we will)
the night is passing.
We'll be responsible, then;
what if he doesn't die from us?,"
they say the men said.
[Xan Malin is set upon]
So there was one man who was
more able,
and he arrived, and
he was the first to hit him.
The men got into the tangle, then,
they got angry.

Pero masanil hab' heb' winh
ix och ijan smak'an winh.
Tsab' xikchaj winh t'a k'en machit,

tsab' mak'chaj winh (t'ay te') t'a te te',
kuchilub', k'e'en,
masanil hab' syak' slatuch heb' winh
t'ay winh.
Pero ha winh jun,
komo te chuk winh,
mab'ax telwilaj winh.
Tsab' xikchaj winh t'a k'en machit,
pero (max) max chamlaj winh.
I hanheja' spak sb'a winh.

Ana' te uk'um xo anh winh,
te' chamnak xo winh yuj anh,
hanheja' spak sb'a winh
t'ay heb' winh.
Yuj chi',
pim tob' heb' winh anima chi',
ay tomab' junh ho wanh,
wak wanh heb' winh ix lajwi,
ix k'ichaj smak'an winh.
Pero hab' ek' wal mul yak'an winh
yet' heb' winh.
jun xo b'i ix telwi winh.
Tsab' stekcham winh heb' winh,
tsab' smil heb' winh winh,
t'ay k'en kuchilub'.
Pero hanheja' max chamlaj winh.
Hanheja' yib'xi winh,
ix yilan heb' winh jun,
ix satam sk'ol winh,
komo jantak ix te chok',
xikaj hab' winh
yuj heb' winh.
Ayab' jun k'en tenam

But all those men, they say,
began to beat him.
They say he was chopped with
a machete,
they say he was beaten with clubs,
knives, stones,
everything, they say, they were hitting
him with.
But that man, well,
since he was so powerful,
they say he didn't fall down.
They say he was cut with a machete,
but he didn't die.
And all the same he
defended himself.
Even though he drank so much,
he was really drunk from the alcohol,
all the same he defended himself
from them.
So,
several of the men,
it would be about five men,
six men, he wounded,
they were broken when he hit them.
But even as he was giving it, they say,
to those men,
a little later he fell down.
They say they stabbed him to death,
they say they killed him
with a knife.
But all the same he didn't die.
While he was still moving,
the men saw
that his spirit left him,
since he was so cut up,
chopped up, they say,
by those men.
There is a rock outcrop

t'a yalanh'em
t'a b'a ay tik te pat
b'ajtil ayek' heb' winh chi'.
Te cha'anh, xi.
Haxob' ta' ix ik'naxb'at winh
yuj heb' winh.
Haxob' ta' ix yumnaxb'at winh
yuj heb' winh,
t'ay xchon k'e'en.
Hab' emka winh
t'a jun sat k'en chi
yuj heb' winh.
Haxob' t'ay sat k'en
ha hab' ta' ay jun te te', xi.
Ha hab' ta' hab' kan
nanhal b'ak'chil winh
(t'ay) t'a te',
t'a b'aj ay sat k'en chi'.
Ix emk'och winh t'ay yich k'e'en.
Ix b'at chi heb' winh,
jantak wan smak'ancham winh chi'.
Hab' k'och heb' winh
t'ay emk'och heb' winh
t'ay yich k'en chi jun,
k'ojan xob' pax k'e winh.
Wan spitswixi winh,
wan sk'ex wan winh,
toxo ix k'ex k'ojan winh,
ana' jantak ix utaj winh smak'naxi.

Hab' emk'och heb' winh ta jun,
ix yilan heb' winh to
wan sk'ex wan winh,
Hab' yamchajxikot winh smak'an,

smak'chaj yuj heb' winh junel xo.
(Hab') Tsab' mak'chaj winh
yuj heb' winh.

down below
where that house was,
where those men were.
Very high, they say.
There he was carried
by those men.
there he was thrown off
by those men,
at the highest point of the rock.
They say he was thrown
down the face of the rock
by those men.
There on that face of rock
they say there, there is a tree, they say.
There, they say, stayed
half of the flesh of that man,
in the tree,
where the rock face is.
He fell to the base of the rock.
The men went there,
the many men who beat him.
When the men arrived,
where they came down
to the base of that rock,
they say he was sitting up again.
He was waking up,
he was changing,
he was even sitting up,
and with all they had done
to beat him.
They say those men went down,
they saw that he still
was changing.
They say they started beating
him again,
he was beaten by the men once again.
They say he was beaten
by those men.

Jantak te xik(k)aj winh,
hasta elab' spixan winh yuj heb' winh,

pero hanhej wala' yak'an winh.
Sat hab' xi sk'ol winh,
smak'an heb' winh (t'ay)
t'ay yich k'en chi'.
Yalan hab' jun xo winh,
"Ini ix aj sat winhaj Xan
Malin xchami,
ana to te winak winh.
To hawal winh ts'alani,
masanil heb' winh chonhab',
masanil mach syak' mandar winh,
masanil yajal yistsil heb' winh anima
syixtej winh,
xal tik neik ix cham winh.
Ini ix aj sat winh xchami,
ob'iltak winh,"
xchab' winh chi'.
(Hab') Yel hab' xi yok winh,
stek'an winh winh.
Najat hab' k'och winh stek'an winh.
Syamchaj hab' kot winh junel xo
yuj heb' winh,
te mak'naxxi winh.
Yuj chi',
elab' spixan winh chi',
yel snholob' hab' sk'en winh
yuj heb' winh.
Yo,
ix tom ta' hab' xcham winh, b'i'an.
Skan winh t'ay yich k'en chi
yuj heb' winh jun, yos,
skot heb' winh
komo sakb'i hab' och heb' winh.
Kasi jun ak'wal yak' heb' winh
smak'ancham winh.

So much was he chopped
that his heart came out
because of them,
but he was giving it out all the same.
He lost his innards again, they say,
when they beat him
at the base of the rock.
One of the men said,
"Look, big man Xan Malin died.

and he was a great man.
And he said,
all the people of the village,
everyone who is in charge,
all the wives of those men
he toyed with them,
and now he is dead.
Now the big man is dead,
poor man,"
they say he said.
They say his foot went out,
it kicked him.
A long way, it kicked him.
He was grabbed again
by the men,
he was beaten hard again.
So,
the heart of that man came out,
his testicles were torn off
by those man
And,
there, they say, he died, then.
He was left at the base of that rock
by those men, then, and
they came back
as dawn was breaking.
Almost all night they were
beating him to death.

Pero ayuch yilumal (wi) hab' winh
yuj heb' winh,
tato max pitswixi winh,
komo te chuk winh, xi.
Ha xo (t'ay) t'a jun xo ak'wal, xi,
"Tas ol kutok sb'at winh tik ne'ik?
b'ajtil skak'ej winh?
Xal ta may, olonh yamchajok,
olonh b'at peresu,"
xchab' heb' winh.
Entonse,
yak'anab' slolonelal heb' winh.
Ke: "Ha heb' winh mak'ancham
winh chi',
mejor b'at kak'ekkan winh t'a
yol b'e tik,
t'a nanhal yaxlu'um,
t'a b'ajtil sb'at b'e t'a chonhab' tik,"
xchab' heb' winh.
Yos,
ijan xit' skot winh,
pero haxob' sk'och heb' winh
t'a b'ajay winh chi jun,
ijan hab' yik'an chanh winh
heb' winh,
maj k'elaj winh yuj heb' winh,
mab'aj k'elaj winh
xchelan chanh heb' winh.
Yuj chi',
"Tas ts'aj tik ne'ik?
Max b'atlaj winh,
max k'elaj winh ku'uj, tas modo.
Mejor kotok hab'
heb' winh ay snok'al sk'ol tik,
tekan ha heb' winh
ol ik'anb'at winh,"
xchab' heb' winh.

[The aftermath of the beating]
But there was a guard left, they say,
by those men,
in case he revived again,
since he was so powerful, they say.
Then on the next night, they say,
"What will we do to move him now?
Where will we leave him?
If we don't, we'll be arrested,
we'll be taken prisoner,"
they say the men said.
Then,
they say they held a meeting.
So: "Those men who beat him,

better go take him from the road,

to the middle of the jungle,
where the road goes to the town,"
they say the men said.
So,
they went back to him,
but they say when they arrived
where he was, well,
and went to pick him up,

they couldn't lift him,
he wouldn't come up,
when they tried to lift him.
So,
"What do we do now?
He doesn't move,
we can't lift him, in any way.
Better that come, they say,
those men who have animals,
perhaps those men
will carry him off,"
they say they said.

Yos, ha xo heb' winh,   So, those men,
masanil choj, okes chi koti.   all the pumas, coyotes, came.
Haxob' nok' schoj heb' winh chi',   And they say those men's pumas
k'och wal t'a b'aj ay skal   arrived among
heb' winh mak'ancham winh chi'.   the men who had beaten him.
Yos, (haxob') hatob' nok',   So, they say the animals
ik'an chanh winh.   raised him up.
Sk'e wanh winh, b'i'an.   He came up standing, then.
Skot winh t'ak'walil,   They came at night,
pero te pural, xi.   but it was hard, they say.
(te wal) Te al winh.   He was very heavy.
Yuj chi',   So,
junab' nok' choj chi' skuchani,   one of the pumas would carry him,
ayab' nok' syaman(n)i,   one, they say, would grab him,
ayab' nok' yamjinak k'e'   one, they say, would lift him up
t'a yich spatik nok' chi',   onto the back of that animal;
tsolal hab' yoch nok'.   they took turns.
Jab'nhej skot jun nok',   One animal would come a little way,
tsab' k'unb'i nok',   he would get tired, they say,
ts'och jun xo nok'.   another animal would take over.
(Yuj) Hab' chi',   That way, they say,
pural hab' jawi kan winh   by force, they say, he was taken
yuj heb' winh,   by those men,
t'a jun yaxlum chi'   to a jungle
t'a b'aj ay skot b'e t'ay chonhab' chi'. where the road comes to the town.
Ha jun yaxlum chi',   That jungle,
K'atelak sb'i.   K'atelak is its name.
Yuj chi',   So,
ha hab' ta' kan winh   they say he stayed
yuj heb' winh,   because of those men,
t'ay nanhal yaxlum chi',   in the middle of the jungle,
t'a yol b'e.   on the road.
Kan nhej hab' winh jun.   He just stayed there, they say.
Haxob' nok' okes,   Then the coyotes,
haxob' nok' k'ochi,   then they arrived,
haxob' nok' lajchianb'at winh.   then they ate him up,
Masanil sk'apak winh chi hab',   All of the clothes of that man
snhikchitej'el nok' t'a spatik,   were ripped off his back by them;

schinaxb'at winh, b'i'an.

Haxob' ix yistsil
winh winhaj (hab') Xan
Malin chi jun,
winh cham chi',
komo yojtak xob' ix,
tsab' kotkan winh jun semana,
chab' semana uk'el anh
(t'aj) t'ay chonhab',
t'a jun jun k'alu'um,
tsab' b'atkan winh uk'el anh
jun semana,
chab' semana,
ma chekel b'aj ay winh.
Yuj chi',
mab'ax snalaj ix
tato cham winh.
"Ajam ay winh uk'el anh,
to xon ton ichatik winh.
Ayam ay winh,
mato t'a chonhab',
mato ajtil k'alumal ay winh,"
xchab' ix icha tik.
Yuj chi',
ha hab' skan winh t'a jun chi'
yuj heb' winh,
haxo t'a t'ak'walil,
tsab' k'och winh t'a spat chi',
tsab' tob' b'at way winh
yet' ix yistsil.
Hab' t'a t'ak'walil chi' sk'och winh,
sway winh yet' ix.
Jantakam lajwi chiman ak'wal, yos,
skotix winh,
tonhej b'at way winh yet' ix,
ana chamnak xo winh.
Tsab' huji xch'alwi winh,

the man was eaten, then.
[The wife learns his fate]
That wife of
the gentleman Xan Malin, well,

the man who died,
she already knew, they say,
he would go out a week,
two weeks, drinking
in town,
in each aldea,
they say he would stay out drinking
one week,
two weeks,
who knew where he went.
So,
she didn't know
that he was dead.
"He's probably out drinking,
that's the way he is.
Maybe he is,
maybe in town,
maybe he's in an aldea,"
they say she said.
So,
when he was left there
by those men,
that night
they say he would come to his house,
they say he would go to sleep
with his wife.
He would come in the night
and sleep with her.
Along about midnight, then,
he would come,
and just go to sleep with her,
even though he was already dead.
They say he would weave,

tsab' hujo sb'owi lopil winh.
Tsab' say yil tik sk'ael winh chi',
t'a b'ajtil sch'alwi chi',
t'ay t'ak'walil chi',
tsab' kotchi winh.
Ayab' jun yawal winh, (t'a jun)
t'a jun yalanh'em k'alum chi'.
Haxob' sk'och winh yunin winh,
t'ay b'aj ay iloj awal chi'.
Ayab' ek' winh t'a skal yawal chi',
yalan hab' winh t'ay winh yunin chi',
"Ha tik ne'ik k'ik'an to tsin k'ochi,
tik to ayinek' t'ay skal kawal tik.
Manhach chiwlaj,
manh ak' pensar yuj ixim,
tik ayinek' t'a skal ixim,
Ayinek' wil ixim,"
xchab' winh ichatik,
ana chamnak xo winh.
Yuj chi',
haxob' sk'och winh yunin chi'
t'ay spat jun,
yalan winh t'a ix snun,
"Ix wil winhin mam, ayek' winh,
t'ay b'aj ay ixim awal.
Ha ta' ayek' winh,
lachan'ek' winh.
'To ch'a'an wal janik' hin k'ol,
to uk'umin anh.
Yuj chi', k'ik'an to, k'ik'an to
tsin k'ochi,'
xchi winh ichatik t'ay(in),"
xchab' winh yunin chi'.
"He, totonam uk'umanh winh,"
xchab' ix,
komo yojtak xo ix jun
chajtil smodo winh.
Tik ni jun,

they say he would make capixays.
They say he would look for his things
where he spun and weaved,
at night
when, they say, he would come.
They say he had a cornfield,
down below the aldea.
They say the man's son would go out
to look at the milpa.
They say he was there in the milpa,
they say he would speak to his son,
"Now just before dawn I will arrive,
I am here in the field.
Don't be afraid,
don't worry about the maize,
I am here to watch the corn.
I am watching the maize,"
they say he said,
even though he was already dead.
So,
when his son would come
to his house,
he would speak to his mother,
"I saw my father, he is there
where the milpa is.
There he is,
lying face down.
'My stomach is a little distressed,
I'm still drunk.
So, tomorrow, early, I'll arrive,'

he said to me,"
said his son.
"Yes, it's likely he's drunk,"
they say she said,
since she already knew
what his behavior was.
Then,

haxob' t'a jun xo ak'wal chi', yos,
haxob' jun snanhal sk'ab'
winh k'ochi.
Yilan ix ha hab' jun snanhal
sk'ab' winh,
pitan k'e t'a yib'anh nok' sk'u ix.
Komo yojtak tonam ix jun,
ke to ha' sk'ab' winh,
mato tas yutej ix sna'an'elta jun,
"Ha tik ne'ik aj ix kot jun k'ab' tik,"
schab' ix.
Sayan hab' yil ix
to ha' sk'ab' winh.
Sna'an'elta ix, b'i'an,
"Tekan to ha' snanhal
sk'ab' winh ha mam.
Lak'an ha' snanhal sk'ab' (winh).

Tob'an ix cham winh.
Tas ix sk'ulej winh?"
schab' ix.
Yik'an hab' jun k'ab' chi ix b'ian, yos,
skot ix yak' parte t'a chonhab'.
"Ha tik ne'ik to saychaj winh,
b'ajtil ay winh.
Tekan to ay heb' winh
ix mak'ancham winh.
Tekan to ix cham winh,
porke ina jun snanhal
sk'ab' winh tik ix k'ochi,
t'a yib'anh nok' hin k'u'.
Ha ta' ayek'i, ix el hin wayanh
t'ay k'inhib'alil."

Yuj chi',
ha hab' jun senhya chi'
yak' winh,
t'ay ix yistsil chi',

the next night, well,
they say one of his fingers arrived.

She saw it was one of his fingers,

lying there on her blanket.
Since she probably knew
that it was his hand,
or maybe she figured it out,
"Now where did that come from?,"
they say she said.
She looked and saw
that it was his hand, then.
She thought, then,
"Perhaps that is the finger
of the hand of your father.
Surely that is the finger
from his hand.
It must be he died.
What happened to him?"
they say she said.
She took the finger then, and
she came to testify in town.
"Now, he should be looked for
wherever he is.
Perhaps there are those
who beat him to death.
Perhaps he died,
because, look, this finger
from his hand arrived,
on top of my blanket.
It was there when I woke up
this morning."
[Xan Malin's remains are found]
So,
they say a sign
he gave,
to his wife,

yik saychaj ilchaj winh, yos,
yelta jantak masanil (heb' winh)
heb' winh mar'alsel (heb')
jantak heb' winh opisyal
say winh.
Haxob' yilchaj'elta winh jun,
haxob' t'a nanhal yaxlum chi'
ayek' winh.
Pero maj xo ilchaj'eltalaj
wal sniwanil winh chi',
haxo nhej hab' sb'akil winh,
komo masanil hab' nok' nok' chi'
lajchianb'at sb'ak'chil winh.
Yuj chi',
haxo nhej hab' sb'akil winh,
yet' hab' sjolom winh ilchaji.
Ayab' jun xchala winh,
ay(y)ab' slopil winh,
masanil lajtob' ilchaj chi'.
Yuj chi',
yilchaj jun, yos,
b'at jantak heb' winh alkal,
jantak heb' winh entendente
t'a pekataxo.
Ha hab' heb' winh, (xit')
xit' ik'ank'e wan hakta
t'a b'ajtil cham winh chi'.
Yuj chi',
ha hab' ta' aykan jun spixan winh,
t'a b'ajay nanhal yaxlum chi'.
Ha hab' ta' tsijtum tob'
heb' winh anima chi' iljinak winh.
Tsab' awajkot winh t'ay heb' winh.
ayab' b'aj linhanek' winh
t'a yol b'e chi'.
Sjawi heb' winh anima,
hanheja wa yaj winh.
Sk'anb'an winh t'ay heb' winh,

so he would be looked for, and
all the many people,
the mayordomos,
how many of the officials
looked for him.
So he was found,
in the middle of the jungle
he was.
But not found
was much of him,
just his bones, they say,
since all of those animals
had eaten his flesh.
So,
they say that just his bones,
and his head, they say, were found.
They say there was a scarf of his,
there was his capixay,
they say that was all that was seen.
So,
when he was found, and
out went some of the *alcaldes*,
many of the *intendentes*,
from long ago.
They say those men
went out to make an *acta*
there where he died.
So,
they say that one of his spirits
stayed there in the jungle.
They say that many
people have seen him.
They say he cries out to them,
they say he's just standing there
in the middle of the road.
When people come by,
he's just standing there.
He asks them

b'ajtil sk'och winh,
b'ajtil ay heb' winh.
Tsab' lolon winh yet' heb' winh.
Hanejab' wa'kan
jun spixan winh chi ta'.
Yuj chi',
haxob' saychaj ilchaj
masanil sk'ael
winh chi' jun,
ha tob' jun winh sekristario
t'ay chonhab' chi',
ha tob' winh ilan'elta
k'en smedaya winh chi'.
Yuj chi',
yik'an hab' kot k'en
winh sekristario chi',
haxob' t'a b'ajay sway winh.
Haxob' ta' yak'kan winh,
t'a b'a'ay smexa.
Pero haxob' t'a t'ak'walil,
tsab' awaj'och t'ay schikin winh.
"K'eanh wa'an, kon!
Pekatax kan ko b'eyek'i!

Kon!" xchab' t'a winh ichatik
T'ay jun jun ak'wal
tsab' b'uychaj chanh winh yu'uj.
Ek' mul jun, maj techaj yuj winh chi',
jantak ts'awaj t'ay winh, yos,
jun xo syuman'el hab' winh, yos,
(sb'at) slajwel, b'i'an.

Yuj chi',
ichachi' hab' ik'an
xcham winh.
i jantak hab' winh anima chi',
yamchaj tob' heb' winh.
Jay wanh xo heb' winh

where they are going,
where they are from.
They say he chats with them.
So they say that there remains
one of his spirits there.
So,
when there were found
all of his things
of that man, well,
one of the *secretarios*
from town,
he found
that man's medallion.
So,
he took it with him,
that secretary,
to where he slept.
He left it there
where there was a table.
But they say that at night
it would talk into his ear.
"Get up! Let's go!
It's been a long time since
we went out!
Let's go!," they say it said to him.
Every night
they say he was awakened by it.
He couldn't stand it,
so much it cried out to him,
they say he threw it away,
and it ended, then.
[Xan Malin's legacy]
So,
that, they say, is the story
of the death of that man.
And so many people
were arrested.
There were so many men

t'ay yol sk'alum chi',
ay to heb' winh b'at peresu yuj winh.
Ay to heb' winh och peresu.

Pero komo maj wal ilchajok
mach wal mak'an winh,
ichnhej ta' lajwel winh,
yuj chi',
jaye nhej k'ual yak' heb' winh chi',
t'a te presu, yos,
yelix heb' winh liwre, b'i'an.
Yuj chi',
ha winh chi',
aykan yik'ti'al winh.
Te chuk hab' winh.
Tsab' och winh xite'al,
tsab' och winh ixal,
tsab'och winh nok'al,
tsab' och winh
masanil hab' tas syutej sb'a winh.
Tsab' b'at winh sat cha'anh,
tsab' jenhwi winh yet' sniwanil.
Yuj chi', te masanil hab' syal yuj winh.
Yuj chi', ts'ik'an te chuk winh.
Yuj chi',
ha hab' slajwi xcham winh chi' jun,
skuchchajkot winh chi',
tsab' k'och nok' much,
tsab' k'och nok' hostok,
tsab' k'och nok' xulem.
Tsab' sb'ok'uch sb'a t'ay heb' winh.
jantak mak'ancham winh chi'.
Masanil hab' nok' tastak nok'al,
koman k'ochi,
tsab' slatuch sb'a t'ay heb' winh.
Chak xuxum ik',
totonab' manh jantak yek'
t'a skal heb' winh.

from that aldea,
were taken prisoner because of him.
There are still men who were
prisoners.
But since it was not seen
who had struck him,
he just died,
so,
just a few days they spent
in jail, then,
they got out free, then.
So,
that man,
this is his story.
They say he was really powerful.
They say he could be a leaf,
they say he could be a woman,
they say he could be an animal,
they say he could be
anything he could make himself.
They say he could go into the sky,
they say he could fly with his body.
So, everything was possible for him.
So, it happens he was very powerful.
So,
they say when he died,
he was carried off,
they say birds arrived,
they say buzzards arrived,
they say vultures arrived.
They say they fought against
the many men who beat him.
All kinds of animals, they say,
arrived,
they say they hit on those men.
A whirlwind,
so many came
among them.

Tsab' yumji b'eyek'
hab' winh yu'uj.
Hultimo wal k'och jun
smoj yanima winh chi', xi.
Jun k'en k'e'en, xi.
Ay hab' jun k'en k'en
niwan k'och sulsonok,
k'ochab' latnaj k'en t'a skal winh, yo,
smak'an poj k'en hab' heb' winh.
Haxonhej wal hab' jun chi',
xal jun masanil hab' k'ak',
masanil tas k'ochi, xi.
Pero ixo cham winh.
Yuj chi',
totonam ha chi'
ts'ik'an te ay (ay) wal spoder winh,
ts'ik'an te chuk winh,
porke masanil tik ix laj jawi.
Yuj chi',
ha heb' winh mak'ancham winh chi'
laj aljinak paxi,
ke to masanil juntsan chi',
yil heb' winh sk'ochi.
Yuj chi',
ichachi'
chamnak winh anima chi'
b'ajay jun k'alum skuchan
yola kitak chi',
ke tob' te' aj b'al winh.

Weno, ix lajwi.

They say they were thrown
against those men by him.
Last came one of
his spirits, they say.
A stone, they say.
They say there was a stone
a big stone came rolling,
they say it bounced into them, and
they say it struck those men.
Just so they say
there came a great fire,
everything came, they say.
But still he died.
So,
surely
he had his power,
he was really powerful,
because all these things came.
So,
those men who beat him
were all witnesses,
that all this,
they saw it come.
So,
thus
died that man
in the aldea called
Yolaquitac,
who was a great sorcerer.
[Closing]
Okay, that's finished.

CHAPTER 7

The Communists

E L AGUACATE (CHUJ *ONH*, AVOCADO) was a small Chuj community located in the northwestern corner of the Departamento de Huehuetenango, Guatemala, some five miles south and ten miles east of the Mexican borders. Its population today is quite distinct from its population when this story was recorded.

The events discussed in this text, recorded by me on May 5, 1965, took place in March, some three years earlier, circa 1962. This predates by decades the disastrous years of the 1970s and 1980s so amply documented by Chris Krueger (1982), Ricardo Falla (1983), Robert Carmack (1988), and Beatriz Manz (1988), among others, the result of the Guatemalan Army's scorched earth policy designed to break the back of a largely imagined Communist insurrection. As in this story, the sources make it clear that the greater danger to the population was the Guatemalan Army, not the Communist-inspired guerillas. The latter were dangerous mainly because the army would destroy anyone and any place that was perceived as aiding them.

The initial incident described here, the entrance into Guatemala of a few guerrillas from their refuge in Mexico, took place in El Quetzal, a Chuj agricultural community located near the Mexican-Guatemalan border, just south of the Mexican settlement of Tziscao, Chiapas, also a Chuj community. According to what I was told during my field work in 1964–65, Tziscao was first established by Chujs who found it convenient to be out of the reach of Guatemalan officials. Such refugees made convenient use of the border. During the time I was doing field work, a "false priest," an elderly Ladino describing himself as one of the priests "*de antes*," had been making a tidy sum by holding mass "baptisms." Denounced by the official priesthood, he was hiding out on a family farm in Mexico, just across the border from Nentón. He was popular because the Catholic priests would only baptize a person once, and the Chuj looked on the rite as a cleansing ceremony that should be repeated periodically.

What I was told in El Aguacate was that a small number of guerrillas had crossed over into El Quetzal and requested hospitality (*posada*) from a household there. When they departed temporarily for neighboring areas, they left a cache of weapons stored in the house, without sufficiently warning their host of the nature of what they were leaving. The cache apparently included grenades, and it appears that children from the host family got into the cache and detonated a grenade, killing themselves and other members of the household. This was a gross violation of the unwritten rules of hospitality: you did not pay back kindness with harm, however unintentionally. The story of this incident spread quickly. As a result, the locals were none too positively inclined toward the guerrillas.

However, when the army arrived to chase down the intruders, it quickly became clear that they were the greater menace. Under threat of annihilation, villagers were obliged to carry out the search for the guerrillas themselves, and they were told that if the intruders managed to get to their settlements, the army would have to destroy entire villages. In the infamous words of an American officer in Vietnam, it would be necessary to destroy the village in order to save it.

In this case, the intruders were captured far from the aldeas where the story was recorded. The place of capture was called Canán. This may be either a *caserío* of San Mateo Ixtatán occupied by Kanjobal (Q'anjob'al) speakers, or a finca near San Mateo purchased in the 1960s in order to establish an agricultural cooperative by Father Arthur Nichols, then the Maryknoll priest of San Mateo Ixtatán (Hopkins 2012a:116). In either case, it was sufficiently distant from El Aguacate and its neighbors to leave them free from harm. This condition was to last less than twenty years.

The finca San Francisco, mentioned often in this account as one of the three aldeas most concerned, was owned by a coronel in the Guatemalan Army. He apparently became convinced that his workers, who lived in a settlement on the finca, were cooperating with the guerrillas. On July 17, 1983, the army descended on the village. Ricardo Falla (1983) interviewed the few survivors, who fled to refuge in Mexico.

The story of the army atrocity begins with words similar to those of the El Aguacate recollection: "I will tell my brothers here what happened to us there in San Francisco . . ." (Manz 1988:246). The soldiers arrived in the late morning in helicopters, ate the food that was offered them, and then looted the houses and took personal property, divided the women into small groups and proceeded to slaughter them in the most gruesome fashions. Finishing the women, they dealt with the children and then the older men. The remaining men were systematically killed with the exception of some half dozen who escaped, including one who, returning from field work, hid outside the village and watched the proceedings. More than three hundred people were killed (Krueger 1982:15–16).

This incident differs from others mainly in being better documented. A wave of such events swept across the Chuj communities over the next year. By 1984, an official report (PAVA 1984) listed forty-six settlements in northern Huehuetenango that had been abandoned, including El Aguacate, El Quetzal, Yalambojoch, and San Francisco, aldeas mentioned in the present report (Manz 1988:89).

The slaughter and displacement of the Chuj population drove thousands into resettlement camps in Mexico, and many continued on to the United States, where there are sizeable Chuj colonies in several states, some in urban areas (Los Angeles), some in mountainous environments similar to their homeland (western Virginia and North Carolina), and some in agricultural areas (Florida). If there was a positive result of this exodus, the presence of so many refugees drew international aid agencies to Chiapas, and a few years later their presence and acquaintance with the local indigenous populations softened the Mexican government's response to the Zapatista uprising. It was not possible to carry out the Huehuetenango scenario in Chiapas with so many foreign observers looking on.

This recording is one of what I came to think of as "Catholic laments." My principal language consultant and field partner was Francisco Santizo Andrés, a native of San Mateo Ixtatán who was recommended to me by Father Nichols when I first went to San Mateo to begin my dissertation research (Hopkins 1967a). At that time the Chuj Catholic community was a small minority, most people being "pagans," as they are referred to here, that is, traditionalists, practicing a variety of syncretic Christian and native religion. As Oliver LaFarge's contacts in Santa Eulalia told him (LaFarge 1947), they practiced "the whole religion," not just the Catholic or pre-Columbian halves. Francisco had served as a simultaneous translator for the American Maryknoll priest in his sermons and other activities, and he was well acquainted with the scattered congregations of persecuted Catholics.

When we undertook to carry out a dialect survey, moving from settlement to settlement across the Chuj-speaking region, Francisco made use of his connections to procure lodging and food as well as speakers to interview. Soon our hosts became aware that we were carrying a tape recorder (a battery-operated Uher), and they requested the favor of recording and delivering messages to the Catholic groups we would encounter down the road. Many of these were true laments: "Oh, my brothers, let me tell you how we have suffered at the hands of the pagans." This one was not.

The narrator was the head catechist for the Catholic community in El Agua-cate, a man zealous for his flock who had been eyeing me suspiciously, suspecting I was not Catholic. Sitting in on a rosary may have helped him accept me, as well as the arrival of a couple of men from San Mateo, friends of Francisco, one of them the first Catholic convert from El Aguacate. In any case in the evening the catechist (whose name I never got) dictated this story and was pleased with the recording.

The Communists

Narrator: Unidentified (the head catechist of El Aguacate Catholics). Interventions by a second unidentified speaker are translated in parentheses. Other material that is in parentheses but not translated includes false starts and corrected errors and is ignored in the translation.

Location: El Aguacate, Nentón, Huehuetenango, Guatemala
Date: May 5, 1965 (recorded in El Aguacate)
Chuj Text 31 [CAC 002 R036]

Hal tiknek an ermanu yuj yos
ix ja jun lawlador tik
t'a ko kal tik heyet'ok.

Wal b'at ha tikneik, ol wal b'ati,
walelta chajtil (ix) ix k'ulej
t'a jun (b'íb') b'ab'el ix ko k'ulej,
ix och jun k'inh,
jun sk'inh jun inhmajenh tik t'a tik.

T'a wente kwatro de marso.
Ak'to wal janak inhmajenh tik,
mantalaj junh k'inh tsuji ix,
(tik tik) b'ab'elto jun chi'.
Yos, (tik tik) k'okb'il
wal kak'an selewrar jun pyesta
t'a jab' kiglesya tik t'a Awakate tik.
Antonse wal yochkan
yak'an komensar
jun pyesta t'a iglesa El Awakate tik.

Entonse haxo (ixka) ix jawi awiso,
chajtil to wan sja heb' winh
komuniste.
Hab' t'a Ketsal,
t'a prontera.

[Opening]
Now, then, brother, thanks to God
a recorder has come here
among us with you all.
[Evidentiality Statement]
I say, here, I will say,
I'll speak about what we did
the first time we did it;
we made a fiesta,
a fiesta for this saint's image here.
[Background]
It was on the twenty-fourth of March.
Still new was the image,
there still had been no fiesta,
it was the first time.
So, at the same time
we were celebrating a fiesta
in our little church here in Aguacate.
Then it was starting,

the fiesta in the church in
El Aguacate.
[The Communists were coming]
Then already came the news,
how the Communists were coming.

They said at Quetzal,
on the [Mexican] border.

Hata' ix otta heb' winh,
ay jun te pat
b'aj ix way heb' winh ta',
ix k'an sposao heb' winh t'a jun
te pat chi'.
Tikni jun ix yak'kan jun
juisyo heb' winh
t'a jun te pat chi',
to yik komo yet'nak armamento
heb' winh.
Yos, por pawor yik winh aj pat,
ix ak'nax sposado heb' winh.
Manh yojtakok winh powre chi jun
tato kontra heb' winh,
kontra gowyerno heb' winh tik.
Ni tob'an tsok kontra gowyerno
heb' winh ix otta,
tob'an komunista heb' winh.
Tikni jun ix lajwikan'el winh
aj pat chi',
yet' spamilya.
Yos, ha Watemala.

Hachi' wan sk'anb'an heb' winh
b'ajtil ay sb'e'al yet' Sam Mateo.
Ha wal chi' wal yak' eksijir
heb' winh,
hachi' wal sk'anb'ej heb' winh,
b'aj ha wal chi',
b'aj wan sb'at heb' winh,
yet' t'a Wariya.
Pero manhok wal t'a puewlo chi'
wan sb'at wal heb' winh,
komo tonhej wan yak'ankan
kumrar chi'
heb' winh ha t'ay Kanan.
Hata' wan st'inhb'itanb'at sb'e
heb' winh.

There they entered;
there is a house
where they slept there,
they asked for lodging at that house.

Later they did an injury

to that house,
because they had armaments
with them.
So, as a favor from the house owner,
they were given hospitality.
The poor man didn't know
that they were enemies,
enemies of the government.
They were against the government,
those men who came in,
they were really Communists.
Later the house owner was left dead,

with his family.
And this is Guatemala.
[Where they were headed]
What they were asking was
where was the road to San Mateo.
That is what they were demanding,

that is what they were asking for,
where it was,
where they were going,
and to Barillas.
But it wasn't to that town
they were going to,
since they were just heading up,

those men, to Canán.
To there were they directing
their road.

Yujchi', topax k'okb'il
wal yoch (jun jun) jun pyesta t'atik
yik inhmajenh Sanh Grawyel tik
t'Awakate tik.
Yo, ix te xiw sk'ol anima
t'a jun chonhab' tik,
yet' t'a B'ojoch,
yet' Samran.
Ha wal oxe' aldea tik te triste.
Ix aj t'a jun tiempo
t'a wente kuatro de marso chi',
tekan to yoxil hab'il na'ik.
Ix el t'a marso pax tik.
(Tekanto yoxíl)

Entonse,
te triste ix aj oxe aldea tik.
Haxob' tikni jun,
haxo ix ko na'an Awakate honh,
to ha tik ol ja heb' winh,
ix laj el heb' winh jantak
topax k'okb'il
yochkan jun k'inh jun.
Haxo (ix . . .) haxonhej
katolika tik jun,
komo ay jun sk'inh wan yochi,
haxo ix yak' preparar sb'a,
skan t'a iglesa tik, (yet') yet'
sk'inh chi'.
(Maxil to ix hulonh skach heb' winh
yet' te aj jun,
maj stak' heb' winh yel te aj.)
Maj, maj,
topax ha heb' winh pagano ayuch t'a,
topax ha heb' winh pagano,
ayuch t'a jusgado tik jun,
ha heb' winh ayuch empleadoal.

[People were frightened]
So, at the same time, people
were about to make a fiesta here
for the image of San Gabriel,
in Aguacate.
So, people were very frightened
in this town,
and in Yalambojoch,
and in San Francisco.
Those three aldeas were very sad.
It was about the time
of the twenty-fourth of March,
maybe the third year ago now.
It emerged in March again here.
(Maybe the third [year ago].)
[The fiesta is threatened]
So,
very sad were the three aldeas.
They say that then,
when we thought we here in Aguacate
that they would come,
how many people left at the time

the fiesta began.
When only we Catholics were here,

since there was a fiesta beginning,
when it was being prepared, they
stayed in the church here, with
that fiesta.
(They didn't see that they came to
silence us because of the fireworks,
didn't want the rockets to go up.)
No, no,
it was the pagans that came here,
it was the pagans,
that were in the city hall (*juzgado*),
those who were officials (*empleados*).

"K'alok yat to ix yak' nular
jun pyesta t'a iglesa tik,"
yalan heb' winh opisyales t'a
jusgado tik.
Cha'el oxel ix hulek' heb' winh
(tik tik) yak' reganyar katolika
t'a iglesa tik, tik ni jun.
Pero maj yak'laj respetar katolika.

Por ke yojtak katolika jun,
to ladinu heb' winh chi'.
Tekan yo, ay b'aj ts'ek' heb' winh

t'a (t'a) pueblu grande ay iglesa.
Klaro yaj t'a yol niwak chonhab',

Yuj chi, jun hachi' ix yekxi
sna' katolika tik,
"Ma'ay, manh olonh el laj.
Komo
(Hatik sko molb'ej ko b'a
t'a ko tepan xkochi . . .)
hatik ol ko molb'ej,
hatik ol ko molul ko b'a t'a tepa tik,

komo ichachi' yalankan
(tik tik) ko Liwru.
Ichachi' yalan Liwru t'ayonh,
t'ayonh jun, ol kak'cham ko b'a
t'a b'ajay iglesa.
Tato, wach'chotonam
tsonh slajel heb' winh,
tato chuk wan ko k'ulani,
tato may jun, tope ma'ay.
Tope ha jab'ok skomwida
heb' winh ol kak'a'."
Kochi, komo triste ton
honh ajxi jun,

"Hopefully they have cancelled
the fiesta in the church here,"
said the officials from city hall.

Two or three times they came by
to scold the Catholics
in the church here, then.
But the Catholics didn't
respect them.
Because the Catholics know, then,
they are Ladinos.
Perhaps there are places they
would pass
in big cities where there are churches.
Clearly there are in the big town.
[The Catholics decide to stay]
So, then, began to
think, the Catholics,
"No, we won't leave.
Since
(We will just gather together
in our church here . . .)
Here we will gather,
here we will gather ourselves in
the church,
since thus says
our Book.
Thus the Book says to us,
to us, we will die to ourselves
where the church is.
If, well hunkered down
they kill us,
if it is bad that we do,
or not, perhaps not.
Perhaps something to eat
we will give them."
We said, as very sad
we were, then,

ix laj el jantak pagano puewlo tik jun,   that so many pagans left the
                                                 town here,
t'a aldea tik.   in this aldea.
Ix laj eli.   They all left.
Wach' jantak (wach' . . .)   Although so many . . .
(Haxo t'a tík ix ko molkut ko b'a.)   (Already we gathered ourselves.)
Wach' jantak winh te' entendido   Although so many of them, very
                                                 intelligent
ix yak' sb'a,   they made themselves,
wach' jantak winh te rasonawle.   although so many are rational.
Pero hasta ix b'atkan winh   But they even went with their luggage,
yet' smaleta,
ix ay winh te najat ix b'ati.   there were some who went far away.
Ha'onh xo tik jun,   And we, well,
kontenta kaji,   we were content,
yet' ko pamilya, yet' kistsil,   with our family, with our wives,
yet' kixal.   with our women.
(T'a iglesa tik   (Here in the church
honh jakan ha'onh tik.)   we came to stay.)
Hatik ay jun alegriya.   Here there was happiness [a
                                                 large crowd].
                                                 [The fiesta begins]
Yos,   So,
b'at kuete (t'a) t'a iglesa tik   skyrockets went up from the
                                                 church here
t'Awakate tik.   in Aguacate.
Ana' ay jun juisyo wan yuji.   And there was a legal decision
                                                 being made.
Ayek' wan sb'éyek' hu'um   There were papers going around
yuj heb' winh (t'a) t'a oxe' aldea tik.   because of the people of these
                                                 three aldeas.
Ix b'at ab'ix,   Notice went out,
ix yak' telegramu heb' winh   a telegram was sent by them
(t'a) t'a B'u'ul, t'a Grasya Dios.   to Bu'ul, to Gracias a Dios.
Ix k'och t'a Nentonh, ix wan sjawi   It arrived at Nentón, they
                                                 were coming
heb' winh yajal t'a chi' ana' wan   those men who were there, and
(trikno)   (trikno [meaningless mistake])

tik ni tob'an t'a (sam) Sam Fransisko.
hata' ix k'och (winh) winh
komuniste.
T'a mismu ora yoch k'inh
t'a Awakate tik.

Yuj chi',
te triste heb' winh,
"Ma'ay, manh xo he yak'el te aj."

(Haxot . . .)
Haxota sna'an ha tik nek jun,
komo dos kosa ol ajok:
"De repenta ha' ol sna'an heb' winh,
heb' winh sollao fuersa gowyerno
t'a Watemala,
to ha heb' winh wan yak'an tronar

t'a aldea tik.
Entonse ha junh womwa
wien ol yak'em
heb' winh t'a yib'anh aldea tik.
Ol lajwel chonhab'."
Ichachi' ix yal heb' winh opisiales,
heb' winh pagano t'ayonh.
Ix ja heb' winh t'a iglesya.
"Ma'ay. Tom ijan manh
yojtakok heb' winh
chajtil sk'anh te aj jun?"
xchachixi heb' winh katekiste
t'a Awakate tik,
t'a b'ajay iglesa tik,
I lo mismu:
"Ma'ay snatop," [snata] haxo
ix yutejxi
yalan heb' winh opis. Cha'el oxel,
ix hulek' heb' winh opisyal honh
yak' tentar t'a iglesa tik.

really at San Francisco,
that's where the Communists arrived.

At the same time the fiesta started
at Aguacate, here.
[The authorities ban fireworks]
So,
very sad were they,
"Nobody is to send up
rockets anymore."
(Already . . .)
Already they thought, now,
maybe two things would happen:
"So what if they would think,
the soldiers of the government forces
of Guatemala,
it was them who were causing
explosions
in the aldea here.
Then they would drop a bomb

on top of the aldea here.
The town would be finished."
Thus spoke the town officials,
the pagans, to us.
They came to the church.
"No. Could it be those men
don't know
how skyrockets sound?"
said for a second time the catechists
of Aguacate here,
where the church is.
And the same thing:
"They don't know," when they
came again,
the officials said. Two or three times;
the officials came to us
to molest, at the church.

Lo mismu ix cha' alanxi
heb' winh jun,
"Ma'ay snata heb' winh
komuniste chi',
to ha heb' winh fuersa gowyerno
wan yak'an. Wan sjawi.
Aktejek el te aj chi'.
Manh xo he sik'ek te'.
Manh xo he yak' tronar te',"
xchi'xi heb' winh cha'el oxel. (ix
yak' . . .)
Ix yak' halto heb' winh (t'a de) t'a
iglesa tik.
Por eso, yuj chi'.
Pero jun maj yab'laj
jantak anima ay t'a tik,
toton ay heb'
t'a jun (alegre) alegria jun.

Yuj chi',
ix te xiw sk'ol oxe' aldea tik.
Pihor jun haxo ix ja winh koronel,
t'a Watemala.
Ix yalan winh t'a heb'
winh awansado,
ix xit'ek' yak' wijilar
t'a Wajxak K'an Nha tik,
topax hata' ix b'o' kampamente:
"Ma hatik naik,
swal t'ayex, hijo,
tato ayam junh aldea chi'
b'aj ol wanaj heb' winh
komuniste tik,
entonse ay nesesida ol lajwel
jun aldea.
Por ke ke modo manh
ol lajwel junh aldea jun,
toton hata' ol och howal.

The same thing they said again,

"Those Communists don't know

if the government forces
are doing it. They're coming.
Stop sending up rockets.
Don't pick up any more rockets.
Don't explode any more rockets,"
they said again, two, three times.

They halted things in the church here.

Therefore, for this reason.
But they didn't note
how many people were here,
how they were
in a large crowd (a "happiness").
[The Army arrives]
So,
the three aldeas were very frightened.
Worse yet, when a coronel came
from Guatemala.
He told those advance men

who went out to watch
in Guaxacaná,
where they made their encampment:
"Here and now,
I'm telling you all, sons,
if there is an aldea
where those Communists stop,

then it will be necessary to finish
the aldea.
Because how could we not
finish that aldea, then,
if there will be a fight there.

Muchu kuidado hex.
Tato liwre to he yaj tse yila',
tse yil wal sk'ochkan heb' winh
kontra chi'
(t'a) t'a jusgado,
entonse tse b'esel he b'a
yet' jantak he pamilya tam
liwre he yaji,"
xchab' winh koronel
t'a heb' winh komisionado militar
t'a Wajxak K'an Nha tik.

Yuj chi',
icha masnhej ix te xiw ko k'ol,
jantakonh animahonh tik t'a
aldea tik.
Ay nesesida ol lajwel
jun jun aldea tik nek
b'aj ol wanaj heb' winh,
komo hata' ol yilaj sb'a heb' winh jun
ta ol och gerra yuj heb' winh,
entonse ol lajwok.
Ay nesesida ol lajwel jun gera
jun jun chonhab',
jun aldea.
(Portuna jun tato t'a kampu
t'a wera ol ko cha ko b'a
yet' heb' winh jun,
hata' liwre to ol kan . . .)
Tato t'a kampu (ol . . . ol ko)
ol schalaj sb'a heb' winh jun,
ol ko chalaj ko b'ah,
entonse tope kolan ol kan junh aldea.
Ta yala' ta Awakate ol wanaj
heb' winh,
ta t'a B'ojoch,
ta t'a Sam Fransisko,
ol yala' b'aj ol wanaj heb' winh,

You all take care.
If you see you are still free,
if you see those enemies enter

the city hall,
then get out of there
with all your family, if you're free,"

said the coronel
to the military commissioner
of Guaxacaná.
[The village could be destroyed]
So,
thus, how many of us were afraid,
so many of us in the aldea here.

It would be necessary to finish
every aldea here
where they stop,
since if they are seen
a war will begin because of them,
then it will end.
It is necessary to finish the war
in each town,
each aldea.
(Good luck, then, if in the fields
outside we find ourselves
with them,
if we are still free . . .)
If in the fields
we find them, then,
if we find ourselves there,
then maybe the aldea survives.
Perhaps they will stop in Aguacate,

there in (Yalam) Bojoch,
or there in San Francisco,
will be where they stop,

hata' ol och gera chi'.
E mato B'ulej jun,
mato b'ajtil hatik ne'ik,
"Muchu kuidado hex,"
xchi winh koronel,
ix ja winh t'a winh (komisar)
komisionado militar.

Yuj chi',
(te') ix te xiw sk'ol anima t'a tik
t'a jun tiempo, ay xo
yoxil hab'il chi tik nek,
yuj heb' winh komuniste.
Komo ix yak'kan chamel heb' winh
t'a prontera,
t'a jun lugar skuchanh Ketsal.
Hata' ix jawi heb' winh sjawi,
komo lak'nik skal jun chi'
yet' kolonhya Tsiskaw.
Yuj chi',
te ix xiw sk'ol anima tik jun,
ix milwaj heb' winh tik ni jun.
Ix yamchaj'och trawajo, b'i'an.
(haxo ix) Haxo ix tik ni jun,
ix b'at heb' winh t'a riwa
t'a skuchan B'ulej,
t'a aldea B'ulej,
munisipio t'a San Mateo Istatanh.

Tik ni jun,
te tik maj yamchajlaj heb' winh
t'a aldea tik.
Te wach' (ix yab') ix yab' anima,
te wach' ix yab' chonhab',
aj pat niwak, kotak,
to maj yamchaj heb' winh
t'a aldea.
Hato ta monte ix yamchaj heb' winh,

there the war will start.
And if it's Bulej, well,
or wherever it is now.
"You all be careful,"
said the coronel,
when he came to the
military commissioner.
[The Communists come]
So,
people here were very frightened
at that time, it would be about
the third year ago now,
because of those Communists.
Since they left dead people
at the border,
at a place called Quetzal.
There they came, those who came,
as it's close there to
Colonia Tziscao.
So,
the people were really afraid
they would be killed, then.
Work was started, then.
Already
men went up above
to a place called Bulej,
to the aldea Bulej,
municipio of San Mateo Ixtatán.
[The Communists are captured]
Then,
those men weren't captured
in this aldea.
People were very happy,
the village was very happy,
heads of household, big or small,
that they weren't captured
in the aldea.
Out in the bush they were captured,

tonse ha t'a jun skuchan Kanan,
hata' ix laj ya hata'
ix yamchaj heb' winh.
Manhoklaj t'a puewlo
ix yamchaj heb' winh.
Icha ix kolchaj kan
jantak aldea t'a prontera tik.
Icha ikolchaj xi kan
Samateo Istatanh.
Ham Samateo Istatanh
ol lajwel syal chi',
(ix b'a) ix b'at heb' winh xk'ochi,
tik ni jun.
Yuj yos (maj) maj lajwel ko chonhab',

may aldea ix lajweli chi.
T'a b'e ix yamchaj an chitonab',

ix laj sjulkan'el jun tsanh
sk'e heb' chi' xk'och'i.

Ichachi' ix ko k'ulej t'a jun
tiempo chi'.
Ichachi' yu'uj
ix kak' jun suprimyentu (tax t'a)
tax ix yamchaj'och sk'inh
winh anhjel
Sanh Grawyel tik t'a jun lugar,
aldea hel Awakate tik.
(Telan ayxo yab'ilal jun chi'.)
(ay xo yab'ilal.)
Ay xo.
(Mokx honh ton xiw janík'.)

then in a place called Canán,
there it ended, it was there
they were captured.
Not in the village
were they captured.
Thus were saved
so many aldeas on the border.
Thus saved also was San
Mateo Ixtatán.
If it had been San Mateo Ixtatán
it would be finished
by those men who came,
then.
Thank God our village
wasn't finished,
no aldea was.
On the road where they
were captured,
they fired at some people
who went up there.
[Closing]
Thus we did in that time there.

Thus because of them
we felt a suffering
when we made a fiesta for the angel

San Gabriel here in this place,
the aldea Aguacate, here.
(Certainly it's been years ago.)
(It's been years.)
It has been.
(We really were a bit afraid.)

CHAPTER 8

Taking Out the Salt

T HIS TEXT IS A sample of an extended monologue. It is one of the procedural texts that were dictated to me by Francisco Santizo Andrés in the early days of our work together. In order to get extended samples of speech that I could scan for grammatical and lexical material, I would request that he tell me about some aspect of San Mateo Chuj life. He related a brief conversation with a compatriot he ran across in the Huehuetenango market. He told me about his own life. He discussed maize agriculture. And one day I asked him to tell me about the famous salt trade of San Mateo, the economic mainstay of the town, producing a renowned black salt that is widely sought after for medicinal uses, among others.

The mines lie below the main part of town, between the houses and the river that flows toward Barillas. The area is called *Tits'am* (*ti' ats'am*) "the mouth of the salt." Deep shafts have been dug into the hillside, and the salt at the bottom is in the form of salty water. The salt water is dipped out into pots that are passed up to the surface, and there the liquid is distributed to carriers who take the salt solution to the houses where it will be boiled down into small cakes.

This is no simple matter. The extraction and production of the salt is intricately interwoven into the fabric of San Mateo life. "Chosen men," who have more than usual strength, perform the heavy labor of getting the salt water to the mine heads, but women do much of the surface carrying and the work of boiling down the saline solution. Special clay pots are required for the extraction process, the carrying process, and the process of reduction to salt cakes. The production of these ceramic vessels occupies a considerable population, just as the labor of transportation requires even more labor. Firewood for the reduction process involves another labor force. And marketing the final product is accomplished by local merchants, but entails long-term relationships with buyers from other towns. Care and feeding of the traders and pilgrims who come for the salt from as far away as Mexico adds another source of income.

The salt trade is intimately tied to the local social structure. The right to take out salt at any given time rotates around the population so that in theory everyone gets a chance to profit. On the other hand, certain mines are held by certain factions for their own use, and one mine is the sole property of the chief prayermaker for the town, the alcalde rezador, the *icham alkal* (literally, the "elder-mayor," a term formed by the opposition of "elder," a semireligious office, and "mayor," a political office). These individuals and groups finance their activities and accrue profit by taking out salt. The salt thus supports individual households, neighborhood organizations, civil political officers, and religious groups, the latter traditionalists not affiliated with the Catholic Church. The networks that form through these activities firm up the social structure of the town as well as increasing its income.

The salt mines support important collective activities, and they also provide funds to individual families to pay for advice from diviners. As the narrator remarks, the better the pay, the more favorable the advice given.

One traditional ceremonial round that is supported by funds from the salt is the annual Five Days, the *hoye k'uh*. This period corresponds to the pre-Columbian period called Uayeb in sixteenth-century Yucatán. The Mayan calendar counted eighteen months of twenty days each, plus this period to bring the calendar into rough synchronization with the solar year of 365 days. The days of each "month" were numbered. Alongside this calendar was a divinatory almanac of twenty day names, each representing a supernatural power, that cycled against thirteen numbers that altered each appearance of a day name; this formed a cycle of 260 days that beat against the 365-day calendar. The expected nature of each day was determined by its day number and day name and its place in the solar calendar, in a system in which no combination of these four elements repeated for fifty-two years, roughly the average length of a human life.

When I learned that the day names were still remembered, I asked Francisco, who didn't know all the names, to find out more about this. He himself was a progressive Catholic and a member of the priest's staff at times, but he had a grandmother who was definitely not. He returned from a trip to San Mateo with the news that his grandmother had refused to talk about the day names with him. "What do you want to know that for?" she asked. "You don't believe in any of it."

In neighboring Chiapas, Mexico, the solar calendar survives in many Tzeltal and Tzotzil communities, but the 260-day divinatory almanac has been lost. The opposite is true of most Guatemalan indigenous communities, where the divinatory almanac flourishes, but the solar calendar has beeen abandoned. In Chuj country, the day names are well known and their combinations with the set of numbers is the basis of shamanic consultation. In the story of Oedipus Rex, above (An Old Man Whose Son Killed Him), it is this sort of divination that predicted the fate of the newborn child (and, of course, of his father).

In San Mateo Ixtatán, however, along with the day names there is still one remnant of the pre-Columbian solar calendar, the Five Days, the last calendric period of the solar year. It now falls somewhere around the beginning of Lent, a period in which the Catholic Church tolerates activities like Carnaval or Mardi Gras. Like many year-end ceremonies, the Five Days is devoted to prayers and renewal. On each of the first four days, the traditionalist leaders visit the crosses that mark the conceptual boundaries of the town. This is done in traditional Maya sequence, following the movements of the sun. They gather for food and drink to make preparations; animals are slaughtered for food, drink flows freely, and marimbas play. Then the first day of *hoye k'uh* they go to the east boundary of the town (in the direction of the sunrise, called *ts'el k'uh*, "[where the] Sun exits [the Underworld]"). The second day the group goes to the north boundary, in the direction where the tropical sun reaches its zenith (like the south, the direction is unnamed, as in many Mayan languages; see Josserand and Hopkins 2011). The third day they visit the crosses to the west (*ts'och k'uh*, "[where the] Sun enters"). The fourth day the crosses to the south are visited. Each day, if the crosses need repair or replacement, this is done with ceremony. Finally, on the fifth day, the ancient end of the year, the traditionalists gather in the plaza next to the entrance of the church where there is another cross. More prayers and offerings are made. The performance of this ceremonial round is considered to be necessary for the well-being of the community and its inhabitants. Income from the salt mines funds all these activities (candles, incense, liquor, slaughtered animals, maize foods, and so forth). Thus, part of the economic gain that derives from the salt mines is put to work for the good of the community, a concept that drives the tradition of civil service all over the Maya area.

Note: A version of this text was published in a collection of Mayan texts edited by Louanna Furbee (Hopkins 1980b). That version, done when Mayanist scholars were trying to find out more about each other's languages, includes a transcription of the tape in a technical orthography and a morpheme-by-morpheme glossing of the entire text. The transcription into modern orthography and the translation presented here are new, as is the formatting of the text.

Taking Out the Salt

Narrator: Francisco Santizo Andrés
   Location: San Mateo Ixtatán, Huehuetenango, Guatemala
   Date: September 7, 1964 (recorded in Huehuetenango)
   Chuj Text 8 [CAC 002 R008]

	[Opening]
T'a jun k'utik, ol wala',	Today, I'll talk about
chajtil skutej sk'eta ats'am ats'am,	how we bring up the salt,
chajtil yaj ats'am ats'am (t'ay)	how the salt is
t'ayin chonhab'.	in my town.
Yuj chi',	So,
ol wala' chajtil ts'ikan sk'eta ats'am	I'll talk about how we bring up the salt
t'a pekataxo,	in the past,
i chajtil ts'ikan sk'eta ats'am	and how we bring up the salt today.
tik ne'ik.	

———

	[Background: In the past]
	[The salt comes up]
T'a pekataxo, sk'eta ats'am,	In the past, to bring up the salt,
ay heb' winh t'unhum ch'ub', xih.	there were men called "pot carriers."
Ha heb' winh t'unhum ch'ub' chi',	Those pot carriers
chekel nhej heb' winh, ayuchih,	were chosen men only among them,
porke hanhej heb' winh,	because only those men
te ay yip.	had great strength.
Heb' winh te sik'lab'il,	They were very select men,
heb' winh niwak winak.	they were big men.
Ha heb' winh chi'	Those men
ts'och yik'k'eta ats'am	went in to bring out the salt
t'ay yo'ol chi'	from the bottom there
t'a b'ajtil smolchajih.	where it is gathered.
Porke to, holan	Because there is a hole
t'a b'ajtil ay ats'am.	where the salt is.
B'achkixtak yemih.	It goes down in steps.

———

Yuj chi',	So,
hata ts'em tsolan heb' winh,	there they go down forming a line,

slechk'eta ats'am
t'a yich chi'.
Ay winh sb'ut'an lum ch'ub'
t'ay yich chi',
syak'ank'eta lum winh (t'a winh)
t'a winh ayemk'och chi'
t'ay sb'ab'elal chi'.
Haxo winh xcha'an lu'um,
smeltsaj winh,
syak'ank'eta lum winh,
t'ay winh ayb'at t'a spatik chi'
t'ay xchab'il.
Hanheja' ichachi' sk'ulej winh chi',
masan sk'ehul yuj heb' winh,
t'ay sti' holan chi'.
Haxo winh sekan pax (t'ay)
t'ay sti' chi jun,
Haxo winh sk'echan'elta,
ts'elul t'ay sti' wertah.
Haxota' xekchajih.
Xcha'an winh mach skuchanih.
Porke to,
ch'ok yaj heb' winh
slechank'eta chi'.
Ch'ok yaj pax heb' winh
skuchan kotih.
Yuj chi',
ha heb' winh slechank'eta chi',
ha heb' winh sekan'em
t'a yol xch'ub',
heb' winh skuchankot chi'.

I ha t'a pekataxo,
ay jun tsanh te' kojnub' ch'ub',
te tsikap t'ay pekataxo,
ha te ayem yuj heb' winh ta',
ha ta' syak'uch k'ojan
lum ch'ub' chi' heb' winh.

they dip out the salt
at the bottom there.
There are men who fill the pots
at the bottom there,
they hand up the pot
to those who are down there above
those first ones.
That other man takes the pot,
he turns,
he gives the pot
to the man who is above him there,
to the second one.
Thus they do it,
everything comes up through them,
to the mouth if the hole there.
Another man empties it again
at the door there.
That other man lifts it,
and goes out to the doorway.
There it is emptied.
The man who is to carry it takes it.
Because still,
separate is the man who dips it out,

separate also is the man who carries it.

So,
those men who dip it out;
those men who empty it
into the bottom of the pots,
they carry it away there.

———

And in the past,
there was a wooden pot rack—
cedar, in the past—
that rack was there for them,
there they set down
those pots, the men,

Skuchan lum heb' winh.
I hanheja' heb' winh
skuchankot chi',
sik'b'il tseltah heb' winh,
porke ha heb' winh
te ay yip chi' skuchanih.
Porke tato ha winh malaj yip jun,
max k'elaj skuchan winh,
porke te al.
Porke ha ats'am ats'am chi',
mas te al ats'am t'a yichanh ha ha'.
Ha ha ha', seb'nhej ko k'echan
chanh ha',
xal ats'am ats'am chi jun,
te al ats'am.

Yuj chi',
sik'b'il ts'och heb' winh
skuchan chi'.
Heb' winh slechank'eta ats'am chi',
pax heb' winh slechank'eta
ats'am chi',
siepre ay jab' yik heb' winh.
Porke slajwi slechank'eta ats'am
heb' winh,
syik'an jun jun ch'ub' yik heb' winh.
Pero ha jun jun ch'ub' chi',
jun ch'ub', xchih,
porke te niwan,
ayam jun oxe kintal yalil,

te al.

Yuj chi',
hat'a pekatax chi',
te niwak lum ch'ub'.
Xal tik ne'ik jun,

The men who carry the pots.
And the men who carry the pots there,

chosen are those men,
because those men
great is their strength for carrying.
Because if those men have no strength,
they can't lift it to carry it,
because it is very heavy.
Because that salt water,
salt is heavier than water
That water, easily we can lift up water,

but that salt,
salt is very heavy.

———

So,
chosen they go in to dip it out.

The men who dip out that salt,
and the men who dip out the salt,

always there is a little benefit for them.
Because when they finish
dipping out salt,
they take benefit from each pot.
Because each of those pots,
one pot, they say,
because they are very big,
they are probably three hundred
pounds in weight
very heavy.

———

[Today: Women carry the pots]
So,
in the past,
the pots were very big.
And today, well,

manh xo ichok chi laj,
ix k'exmajih.
Ha tik ne'ik,
ha xo heb' ix
skuchan ats'am.
Porke ha lum ch'ub'
t'ay pekatax chi',
ix lajwel lu'um.
Ha xo lum ch'ub' tik ne'ik,
ha lum kotak xo,
yunetak xo nhej lu'um.

Yuj chi',
oxe' lum chi' (t'a lum)
t'a jun lum niwan.
Porke ha jun lum niwan t'a
pekatax chi',
oxe lum yunetak chi' sb'at t'a
yol lu'um.
Yuj chi',
ha chi' ix poj heb' winh tik ne'ik,
entonse ox ch'ub' ix k'ek'ochih.
Yuj chi',
ox ch'ub' jun jun kantaroh.
Jun ch'ub'.
Yuj chi',
ha heb' ix ix chi',
skuchan tik ne'ik
I ha xo b'at lechchajk'eta
t'a yol chi jun
ha heb' winh winak chi'
b'at lechank'eta t'a yol chi jun,
heb' winh mayor,
heb' winh polinsiah.
ha heb' winh b'at lechank'eta t'a
yich chi'.
Mach smananih,
entonse sinhkwenta sinhku sentawu

they aren't like that any more,
they are changed.
Today,
those women
carry the salt.
Because the pots
in the past,
they have ended.
Those pots today,
they are small already,
just little baby pots.

———

So,
three of those pots
to one big one.
Because those big pots of the past,

three little pots go into their bottom.

So,
then, the men today divided them,
so three pots came out.
So,
three pots, each *cántaro*. One pot.

So,
those women there,
carry them today.
And so, those who go dip it out
from the inside,
those men who
go dip it out of the insides
are those more important men,
the policemen,
those men go dip it out at the bottom.

Whoever is buying
then [pays] fifty-five centavos

jun jun ch'ub'.

each pot.

————

Yuj chi',
ha heb' winh slechank'eta chi',
sentawu skotup jun jun ch'ub'.
Tato jun ch'ub' entero niwan skik'a',
entonse oxe sentawu skotup
heb' winh,
yik heb' winh lechwajum.
Ha xo heb' ix ix chi',
skuchank'eta jun, sja' t'a ko pat,
hoye sentawu sko tup heb' ix.
Tato najattak ayonh, ha chi',
syala jantak b'aj ayonh.
Tato najat ayonh,
mas niwantak sko tupu'.
Ay t'ay (t'ay) siete ocho sentawu,

hasta ay t'ay dies sentawu.
Tato lak'an ayonh jun,
ay t'ay oxe sentawu,
t'a chanhe sentawu.

So,
to those men that dip it out,
one centavo we pay for each pot.
If it's a whole big pot they bring out,
then three centavos we pay them,

the benefit of the dippers.
Also to those women
who carry it, who come to our house,
five centavos we pay the women.
If it's far where we are, then,
we talk about how far to where we are.
If it's far where we are,
we pay more.
There are some for seven,
eight centavos,
up to ten centavos.
If it's close where we are, well,
there are some at three centavos,
at four centavos.

————

Yuj chi',
hata' syala' jantak b'aj ayonh.
B'at yak'ankan heb' ix t'a ko pat,
sko tupan heb' ix.
Sk'och ats'am ats'am (t'ay) t'a ko pat,
ay jun te ko jukib',
hata' ts'em ats'am.
Sjakan ats'am,
skik'ankot te k'atsits,
sko manan lum lu'um
b'ajtil ol ko payej ats'am.
Tato jun ch'ub' ats'am,
jun nhej lum sko mana',
yet' jun xo lum yune nhej.

[The salt is boiled down]
So,
there we talk about how far we are.
They go to leave it at our house,
we pay them.
When the salt arrives at our house,
there is a wooden trough,
there the salt goes down.
When the salt arrives,
we gather firewood,
we buy ceramics
where we will heat the salt.
If it is one pot of salt,
we buy just one vessel,
and just one other little pot.

Tato cha ch'ub' ats'am jun,
entonse chab' lum sko mana'.
I siempre hanheja sko man
jun lum yune nhej chi'.
Porke yik sti'.

Ts'el ats'am ko payanih,
b'at ko chonhan ats'am,
e tato ay winh manum ats'am,
ts'ek pax t'ay kal pat jun.
Ay heb' winh, heb' winh hula',
ha heb' winh smananb'at
ats'am t'ayonh,
t'a pilonhal.
Snunal smanb'at ats'am heb' winh.
Porke ha ats'am ats'am chi',
nab'a ha' ats'am.
Hato sko payan ats'am,
hatota' swinakej sb'a ats'am,
i sk'enan sb'a ats'am.
Yos, (ts'och) b'o jun nun ats'am.

Pero hat'a yik heb' winh
peka winak,
ay skostumra heb' winh.
Hasta hanheja' tik ne'ik,
syak' kostumra winh yet'ok.
Porke winh icham alkal,
ha winh ayuch lesalil,
yak' slesalil masanil ats'am ats'am.
Yak' slesalil heb' winh chonhab',
yak' slesalil masanil awal,
masanil ixim,
masanil trawaju.
Ha winh ayuch yak' slesalil
tato may junh ilya

If it's two pots of salt, well,
then two vessels we buy.
And always even so we buy
just one little pot.
Because its mouth is right.

———

[Buyers come for the salt]
The salt comes out as we heat it,
we go sell the salt,
and if there are salt buyers
they come around the houses.
There are men, Kanjobals,
those men buy the salt from us,

in lumps (*pilones*).
In "mothers" they buy the salt.
Because that salt,
it's pure liquid salt.
So we heat the salt,
then the salt forms a solid,
and the salt turns to stone.
So, it makes a "salt mother."

———

[Ritual surrounds the salt]
But with the men of the past,

there was a custom of theirs.
Even up until today,
they make rituals with it.
Because the alcalde rezador,
that man prays,
he prays for all the salt.
He prays for the men of the town,
he prays for all the fields,
all the maize,
all the work.
That man prays
that there be no harm

ts'och t'ay yol chonhab'.

Yuj chi',
hanheja' ay skostumra heb'
winh yet'ok.
Pero ha winh icham alkal chi',
ha heb' winh chonhab',
ha heb' winh smolan yik
skantela winh,
yik spom winh,
yik staj winh,
yik b'aj syak' lesal,
ana ch'ok yaj jun yats'am winh,
wal ayuch (t'ay) t'ay semanail.
Ha winh ay yik xch'okojil,
ha winh sjakani munil,
ha winh xcha'an stojol,
yik winh sch'okojil.
Yuj skostumre winh chi',
ay jun yats'am winh chi'
t'a xch'okojil.

Xal ats'am spukax
t'ay heb' winh chonhab' chi jun,
chab' nhej ats'am.
Ha ats'am Yochul, xih.
Ha tun atz'am
meru wal mayor minax chi'
yet' ats'am Snanhal, xih.
Ha ats'am Yochul chi',
jun jun k'uh,
sk'eta jun wake kantaro.
Wak ch'ub', jun jun k'uh.
Xal ats'am Snanhal chi jun,
ha to t'ay xchanhlajunhejial,
t'ay yolajunhejial,
hatota' ts'el ats'am.
Pero ts'elta jun holajunh ch'ub',

that comes to the town.

———

So,
just so there have their rituals.

But that alcalde rezador,
the men of the town,
they collect money for his candles,

for his incense,
for his pine shavings,
for whatever he prays for,
and set apart is a salt mine for him,
it is there every week.
He has a benefit set aside
he goes in to work,
he has his own pay,
his benefit apart.
According to their custom,
there is one salt mine for him,
set aside.

———

And of the mines distributed
among the men of the town,
there are only two salt mines.
The mine Inside, they call it.
That mine
is the very best mine
and the mine Middle, they call it.
That Inside mine,
every day
comes up about six *cántaros*.
Six pots, every day.
And the Middle mine,
every fourteen days,
fifteen days,
salt comes out.
But some fifteen pots come out,

jun waklajunh ch'ub'.
Ha heb' winh ichamtak winak,
t'a yol chonhab',
ha heb' winh chi'
ayuch t'a yujal,
yik'an ats'am masanil yempu.
Ha heb' winh chi'
ts'och t'ay ats'am Snanhal chi' . . .

some sixteen pots.
The elders
in the town,
those men
go in monthly,
they take out salt all the time.
Those men
go in to the Middle mine . . .

———

[Tape ends; a new tape begins]

———

Yuj chi',
ichachi' yaj ats'am ats'am chi'.
Pax heb' winh opisyal,
heb' winh ayuch t'ay jusgadu,
siempre syik' ats'am yik heb' winh.
Malaj stojol heb' winh,
hanhej serwisyo heb' winh
syak' t'a yol schonhab'.
Yuj chi',
ha heb' winh chi',
jun jun semana
syik'an oxtak ch'ub' ats'am
yik heb' winh.
Ha jab' chi' stojol heb' winh yajoh,
yik b'aj ts'elta sgasto heb' winh.
Pax heb' winh chi',
ay pax skostumra heb' winh.
Te niwan skostumra heb' winh chi',
porke yik t'a b'ajtil
may tas kot t'a yib'anh heb' winh,
t'ay k'inh,
t'ay (jan) tastak sk'ulej heb' winh.
May jun howal,
may tas ih.

[The officials take salt]
So,
that's the way the salt is.
And the officials,
those who are at City Hall,
always take salt for their benefit.
They don't get a salary,
it's just their service
that they give to their town.
So,
those men,
every week
take out three pots of salt each
as their pay.
That little bit is their pay,
where they take out their expenses.
And those men,
they also have customs.
They make really big rituals
so that
nothing comes down on them
in fiestas,
in whatever they do.
No fights,
no nothing.

———

Yuj chi',

So,

hata' syak' kostumra
yuj yik chi'.
Ha heb' ix yistsil heb' winh yob'sial,
syak'an (e) ja'at heb' ix.
Smolchaj heb' ix,
syak'an jun tsijtum lesal heb' ix.
Sb'at heb' ix t'a tits'am t'ay jun k'uh,
jun k'uhal sb'at heb' ix
yak' lesal t'ay sti ats'am ats'am.
Slajwi heb' ix t'a sti' ats'am
ats'am chi',
sb'at heb' ix t'ay kulus,
t'ay titak chonhab'.
Ixtota' sk'och heb' ix t'a tepan.
T'a jun xo k'uh, ak'wal to,
sb'atxi heb' ix,
sk'och heb' ix t'ay yamak'il tepan,
t'a yib'anh jun kulus.
Haxota' syak' lesal heb' ix
ts'ek' k'uh.
Yob'xial, syak'an jun chi heb' ix,
yik t'a b'ajtyil malaj tas kot
t'a yib'anh heb' winh.

Yuj chi',
ha heb' winh chi'
wal ts'ak'an tsijtum kostumra
yet' ats'am ats'am tik.
Ha heb' winh ts'ak'an jun
kostumra chi',
yik t'a b'ajtil malaj mach
sb'at peresu,
malaj mach ts'ak'am jun es palsoh
t'a yib'anh heb' winh.
Yuj chi',
ha chi' syak' slesalil heb' winh.
Pax heb' ix ix chi jun,
slajwi jun yik heb' ix chi'

there they do rituals
for their benefit.
The wives of the officials,
they make rituals.
They are gathered,
they make some prayers.
they go to the salt mines one day,
one whole day the women go
and pray at the mouth of the mine.
Finishing at the mouth of the mine,

they go to the cross
at the edges of the town.
Thus they arrive at the church.
The next day, early in the morning,
they go again,
they arrive at the patio of the church,
at the foot of a cross.
There the women pray all day.

Every five days, they do this
so that nothing comes
down on them.

———

So,
those men
are making a lot of rituals
with the salt.
They make one ritual

so that none goes to jail,

none makes false testimony
against them.
So,
thus they make their prayers.
And those women,
when they finish praying

t'a masanil,
syak'an yik heb' ix.
Tato yojtak heb' ix
ayuch winh yichmil heb' ix
(t'ay) t'a jusgadu,
entonse ha heb' ix chi',
syak' lesal heb' ix.

Pero ay jun b'ajtil
sk'anb'ej yaw heb' ix,
chajtil syutej slesal heb' ix.
Hata' winh aj chum,
t'a ix aj chum,
hata' sk'anb'ej yaw heb' ix.
Ha chi',
b'at sk'anb'ej yaw heb' ix
tato may tas kot yib'anh heb' winh,
tato may peresu,
may multu,
entonse ha chi' b'at sk'anb'ej
yaw heb' ix.
Haxo winh aj chum chi jun,
ts'em jun wente sinhku,
jun k'en sinhkwenta sentawu
scha winh.
Yos, ol lolon winh,
ol yik'tian winh chajtil yajih.
Tato malaj k'en jun,
ha nhej jun k'en yes sentawu,
jun k'en kinse,
max lolonlaj winh sik'lab'il,
max wal yallaj winh
chajtakil yajih,
porke to jab'nhej k'en tumin.
Tato niwantak k'en jun,
entonse masanil ol yal winh,
sik'lab'il ol yik'ti'ej winh

for everything,
they do it for themselves.
If they know
there is a husband of theirs
in jail,
then the women
pray for him.

———

[Diviners are consulted]
But there is a place where
they ask for advice,
for how to make their prayers.
To the male diviner,
to the female diviner,
there they go ask for advice.
Thus,
the women go to ask for advice
so there is nothing that befalls the men,
so there is no prisoner,
no fine,
then they go ask for advice.

And that diviner, well,
he takes twenty-five,
some fifty centavos
he takes.
And, he will speak,
he will tell them how it is.
If there is no money,
only some ten centavos,
some fifteen,
he doesn't speak well,
he won't say
how things are,
because it's too little money.
If it's a lot of money,
then he will say everything,
he will say choice things

chajtil ol ek' opisyu chi'.
Yuj chi',
ay yik'ti'ej winh,
chajtil ol aj opisyu chi'.

Yuj chi',
ay skostumrail jun chi',
ay slesalil,
eh,
pax heb' winh anima chi jun,
jantak heb' winh chonhab',
ay jab' jab' yats'am heb' winh
chi syik'a'.
Pero ha heb' winh chi',
t'ay partidual ay yuj heb' winh.
Ay jun partidu,
jay wanh sb'eyih.
Entonse, ay jun wajxak wa'anh,
jun lajun wanh heb' winh,
ts'ik'an ats'am ats'am t'a yujal.
Ha tun heb' winh yichamtak
winakil chi',
ha xo heb' winh
jantak to wan sk'ib' jun,
wan yoch yet' heb'winh,
wan sts'akwan yet' heb' winh,
ha heb' winh chi',
t'ay xchab'il, t'a yoxil ujal,
syik'an jab' yats'am heb' winh.
Porke ay b'aj ay
smol tuminal yuj heb' winh.
Tato ay jun tas sna'elta heb' winh,
smolb'anh sb'a heb' winh,
syak'an mol tumin heb' winh.
Smolchaj k'en tumin,
syalaneb' winh b'ajtil sk'och k'e'en.

about how the office will go.
So,
there is a conversation
about how the office will be.

———

[Political factions take salt]
So,
they have their customs,
there are prayers,
and,
again those people,
how many men of the town,
have a little salt they take out.

Because those men,
belong to factions.
There is a faction. for
however many people.
So, there are some eight people,
some ten people,
who take out salt monthly.
And those elders,

and those men,
who are growing up,
they go in with them,
they join with them,
those men
every second, every third month
take out a little salt.
Because there is a time when
they gather money for themselves.
If they are thinking of some thing,
they gather together,
they make a collection of money.
The money collected,
they talk about where it will go.

Tato t'a winh icham alkal
sb'at tumin,
e mato ay jun skostumra heb' winh,
ol yak' t'ay yol yik t'a xch'okojil jun.

If it goes to the alcalde rezador,
and if there is some ritual of theirs,
they put aside money for it.

———

Ichok syak' heb' winh
t'ay hoye k'uh.
T'a hoye k'uh, jantak heb' winh
yichamtak winakil jun jun partidu,
ay (winh) winh sat,
t'a b'ajtil smolchaj heb' winh.
Ha ta' syak' jun sja'at heb' winh,
syak' lesal heb' winh,
syak' jun tsijtum kostumra
heb' winh.
Molchaj heb' winh,
ts'och son,
xcham nok' kalnel,
syuk'an anh heb' winh,
jantak tas sk'ulej heb' winh.

[The Five Days]
Thus they do
on the Five Days.
On the Five Days, however many
elders of each faction,
they have a chief,
where they gather.
There they make rituals,
they pray,
they make a lot of ritual.

Once they are gathered,
the marimba comes in,
a goat dies,
they drink alcohol,
however many things they do.

Yuj chi', semra
ay slesalil jun ats'am chi'
yuj heb' winh,
porke hat'a jun hoye k'uh chi',
ha ta' ay smodo heb' winh,
yawan kulus.
Ha ta' hoye k'u chi',
ha ta' ts'el heb' winh
ichamtak winak
t'ay yol chonhab' chi',
t'ay b'ajtakil ay jun kulus,
t'a b'aj ay jolomtak wits.
B'at yak'an lesal heb' winh,
t'ay sk'inhib'i hoye k'uh.
Tato k'axo kulus chi',
syawanxi heb' winh,

So, always,
there are prayers for the salt
on their behalf,
because on the Five Days,
then they have the custom
of planting a cross.
On those Five Days,
then the elders go out

to the center of the town,
to wherever there is a cross
where there is the peak of a hill.
They go to pray,
on the dawn of the Five Days.
If the cross is rotten,
they plant it again

t'a jun k'u chi'.
Yuj chi',
ha ta' syawej jun tsanh kulus chi
heb' winh.
Porke ha (jun) jun tsanh k'u chi',
mas te niwan t'ay heb' winh,
mas ay swale,
porke yik kostumre yajih.
Slajwi yawan jun tsanh kulus chi
heb' winh,
tato sk'aeli,
e hanheja' t'a jun xo hoye k'uh,
hatota' ol yawej pax heb' winh
jun xo sk'exul jun sk'ael chi'.
Manh komonlaj syawej heb' winh,
masanil yempuh.
Komo ha jun hoye k'u chi',
jun jun hab'il ts'ek'ih,
jun jun hab'il ts'ek'ih.
Yuj chi',
ha jab' slesal
heb' winh ichamtak winak chi',
ha jab' chi', sb'o heb' winh.

Yuj chi',
ayuch heb' winh,
t'a yujal yik' ats'am ats'am chi',
chatak ch'ub' syik' jun jun.
Ayam junok kwarenta homre
heb' winh,
ts'ik'an ats'am,
chatak ch'ub' chi'
t'a jun jun uj.

Yuj chi',
ichachi' yet'nak yik ats'am
ats'am chi'.

the next day.
So,
they plant some crosses.

Because on those days
it goes better for them,
it is of more value,
because of the benefit of the ritual.
They finish planting some crosses,

if they are rotten,
and if it's so the next Five Days
then they will plant again
another replacement for the rotten one.
It's not usual that they plant things
all the time.
Since that Five Days
comes every year,
every year it comes to pass.
So,
they pray a little
those elders.
a little bit they do.

———

So,
among those men,
monthly they take salt,
two pots each they take.
There are about forty men

taking out salt,
two pots each
every month.

———

[Closing]
So,
that's the way it is with the salt.

APPENDIX I. A SHORT SKETCH OF CHUJ PHONOLOGY, GRAMMAR, AND SYNTAX

Phonology

Chuj is a typical Mayan language in that it has a series of glottalized stops and affricates that parallel a set of plain consonants. It is unusual in preserving the velar nasal (*nh*) and an ancient contrast between velar and laryngeal fricatives (*j* and *h*, respectively) that has been lost or transformed in most languages. The velar nasal written *nh* is pronounced like the English *ng* as in *sing*, but unlike English *ng* it also occurs in word-initial position, with the same pronunciation. The velar fricative written *j* is pronounced like the Spanish consonant *j*, a voiceless velar fricative, similar to German *ch* in *ach!* The Chuj consonant *h* is not pronounced as a voiceless vocoid as it is in many languages, but as a voiced vocoidal onset or offglide of the same vocalic quality as the adjacent vowel (that is, *ha'* "water" sounds like [aá']). In a sense it is just a lengthening of the vowel, but it carries with it a deep rasp that merits its designation as a laryngeal fricative. In word-final position it is essentially lost phonetically; while it can be argued on structural grounds that there is no word that ends in a vowel and underlying *h*s are revealed if vowel-initial suffixes follow, this final *h* is—by convention—not written (although it will appear in morphophonemic transcription below).

A complete inventory of significant phonological units would include not only consonants and vowels, but stress, contour, and juncture phenomena as well. For a fuller discussion of this phonological system, see my dissertation (Hopkins 1967a) or its modernized version in the AILLA archives. The inventory of segmental phonemes is written here with the orthographic conventions of the Academia de las Lenguas Mayas de Guatemala (Lenguas Mayas de Guatemala 1988). Elsewhere (in other presentations of my Chuj material), for greater visibility the glottal stop is written as <7> rather than <'>, and I retain the structurally appropriate symbol <p'> for the glottalized bilabial stop rather than the externally imposed <b'>. The latter consonant is voiceless [p'] in initial and final positions and voiced ['b] only medially; between vowels it is frequently implosive [b"].

The native consonants of Chuj include the following: voiceless plain and voiceless glottalized stops and affricates at labial (*p, b'*), gingival (*ts, ts'*), alveolar (*t, t'*), velar (*k, k'*), and glottal (*'*) points of articulation; voiceless fricatives at alveolar (*s*), alveopalatal (*x*), velar (*j*), and laryngeal (*h*) points of articulation; voiced nasals at bilabial (*m*), alveopalatal (*n*), and velar (*nh*) points of articulation; voiced semivowels at bilabial (*w*), and alveopalatal (*y*) points of articulation; a voiced alveolar lateral (*l*) and an alveolar flap (*r*).

The flap, found mostly but not exclusively in loanwords, varies with the Guatemalan Spanish voiceless retroflex fricative (like the final allophones of *r/rr* in many Spanish dialects). Likewise, *f* and the voiced stops *b*, *d*, and *g* occur only in words taken from Spanish and vary in their articulation according to the acculturation of the speaker.

The vowels of Chuj are high and low front vowels *i* and *e,* low central *a* and low and high back rounded vowels *o* and *u*. Strong stress in words is generally on the vowel of the root, with secondary stress on final syllables. While marking stress is not part of the official orthography and is not necessary for native speakers, in other works—and in the text analysis below—I have added accent marks on the strong syllables to help the nonnative reader appreciate the rhythm of speech.

Most roots are consonant-vowel-consonant monosyllables (CVC), although more complex patterns are not rare (CVCVC, especially CVjVC and CV'VC, and even CVCV'VC). There is a common pattern of alternation between CV'VC and CVC shapes that suggests an underlying *CV'C shape for many lexical items, that is, /lu'um ~ lum/ "earth," /k'e'en ~ k'en/ "stone." Vowel sequences (VV) are relatively rare except where a consonant has been lost in rapid speech, and consonant clusters (CC) occur most frequently at morpheme boundaries.

There are regular morphophonemic reductions in consonant sequences that result from adjacent morphemes: '-C and *h*-C reduce to C alone; C-*h* goes to C except that *b'-h* becomes *w*; *ts-'* becomes *ts'*; word final ' and *h* are frequently lost; *t-x* may become *tch*; *ch-x* becomes *tx* or *tch*. In verbal prefixation, the aspect marker *ts*-becomes *s* before consonants (other than *h* or '), and this *s* assimilates to following *ch* or *ch'* as *xch* and *xch'*.

Morphology

Root morphemes may be classified into some six root classes, although some roots cross class lines and others are difficult to classify. This classification is based on inflectional and derivational affixation, that is, the occurrence of the root with different sets of affixes. Abbreviations in small capitals (TV) are taken from Aissen et al. (2017:vii–x) and include those used in the text analysis, below.

Verb roots are CVC in shape and can be divided into transitive, intransitive, and positional verb roots. Transitive roots (VTR, TV) and intransitive roots (VIN,

ITV) may be inflected for tense/aspect and person (subjects and objects) without derivation, but positional verb roots (VPO, POS) always occur in complex stems.

Transitive verb roots are unambiguously identified by their co-occurrence with the suffixed clitic-*hV'* ~-'*Vh*, -*hV'* (the latter follows roots that end in ', the former occurs elsewhere): *pi'-'ah> pi'ah*, "to take the kinks out of something"; *pih-ha'> piha'* "to stretch something"; *tib'-ha'> tiwa'*, "to carry something cylindrical"; *b'o'-'oh> b'o'oh*, "to fix something"; *b'ol-ho'> b'olo'*, "to roast something"; *ts'ul-hu'> ts'ulu'*, "to peel something." A small set of transitive verb roots do not take these affixes, but take the suffix-*ej*; some verbs may occur with either: *'uk'u'* ~ *'uk'ej*, "to drink something"; *lo'oh* ~ *lo'ej*, "to eat soft things"; *'utej*, "to do something"; *payej*, "to dry maize by heating."

Intransitive verb roots are unambiguously identified by their co-occurrence with the suffixed clitic -*(ih)* without derivation of the CVC root; this morpheme also occurs after derived stems that will be inflected with intransitive affixes. It is realized as -*ih* if no word or phrase follows; otherwise it is deleted: *b'at-(ih)> b'atih*, "to go"; *ts-ø-b'at-(ih)> sb'atih* "someone goes"; *ts-ø-b'at-(ih) winh> sb'at winh*, "he goes"; *cham-(ih)>chamih* "to die"; *ix ø-cham-(ih)> ix chamih*, "someone died"; *ix ø-cham-(ih) winh> ix cham winh*, "he died."

Positional verb roots deal with the specification of positions, shapes, aggregations, and other physical features of objects and people, that is, functions that are associated with adjectives in many other languages: *hap*, "to be a big open hole"; *senh*, "to be circular"; *tonh*, "to be thick and ugly"; *tob'*, "to be a bundle of flexible stick-like things." Some VPO roots are distributive, indicating features that are distributed across a number of objects; others are nondistributive, indicating features that are concentrated on a single object. The two contrast most sharply in derived numeral classifiers: *cha' pots-anh lu'um*, "two dents in a (single) clay pot" [nondistributive]; *cha' pil-anh lu'um*, "two ball-shaped pieces of clay" [distributive].

The sole "existential verb" (VEX, EXIST) is *ay*, to be. It takes only -*an* (extended action, DUR) for derivation and is not inflected for tense/aspect, but can be inflected for subject, negative, intensive, interrogative, and reportative, among others. Inflection for personal subject is like that of stative stems (see below). The morpheme *ay* is not actually a verb; it is an existential predicator that plays the role of a verb in sentence composition, as do stative stems.

Noun roots (N) are of varied shapes, including CVC, CV'(V)C, CVCVC, CVCV'C, and CVCCVC. Spanish loanwords have added myriad shapes to this inventory. Four subclasses of noun roots can be distinguished by distinct patterns of derivation and inflection: substantives, adjectives, numerals, and noun classifiers.

Substantives are difficult to characterize, as they form many minor subsets. In general, substantives are noun roots that may be inflected for person (possession), but not for tense/aspect. In syntactic constructions, substantives are typically preceded by a noun classifier that specifies their inherent nature (that is, functioning like gender markers, but there are more than a dozen "genders"; see Hopkins 2012b for a discussion of their origin). Some substantives do not occur possessed, and some are not associated with noun classifiers.

Adjectives (ADJ) are generally of the shape CVC, but there are some exceptions (that is, *ya('a)x*, green). Adjectives do not take inflection for person or tense/aspect; they are often derived by the desinence *-b'-(ih)* to form intransitive verb stems, that is, *yax-b'-(ih)*, *yaxb'ih*, "to turn green." A large subset of adjectives, the color terms, combine with unique derivational suffixes to describe aspects of color.

Numerals (NUM) are of the shapes CVC, CVCVC and CVCCVC. They may occur underived with affixes of person, forming ordinals, but not with affixes of tense/aspect. They are distinguished from all other classes by their occurrence with a unique set of derivational suffixes to form the names of time periods and cycles. Syntactically, numerals are distinguished by their unique occurrence before numeral classifiers. The Chuj numeral system is vigesimal, based on cycles of twenty. Number roots represent the values one through twelve and even multiples of twenty. All other values are represented by compound stems.

Noun classifiers (NCLF) form a small but syntactically important set of nouns. In general, they are recruited from the set of substantives, but there are exceptions. They have functions like gender markers (determinatives) and pronouns in other languages. As the former, unstressed, they precede nouns referring to material objects to specify the inherent nature of the referents; as the latter, stressed, they substitute for the nouns in contexts where the referent is understood. The inventory of noun classifiers is as follows:

ix, female beings, human or mythological;
winh, male beings, human or mythological, and including some introduced diseases;
nok', animals and animal products;
ixim, maize and other grains and their products;
ch'anh, vines and their products;
te', woody-stemmed plants and their products;
anh, herbaceous plants and their products;
lu('u)m, earth, earthen products, and geographical features;
k'e('e)n, stone, metals, and their products;

k'apak, cloth and cloth products;
ats'am, salt and its products;
ha', liquids and hydrological features;
yab'il, illnesses;
k'inal, rains;
nayleh, sheet-like plastic (<Spanish *nailon*, nylon).

From reports of this system the inventory appears to vary slightly from speaker to speaker. The putative origin of this category, Chiapanec, a neighboring Oto-manguean language, is discussed in Hopkins (2012b); semantic categories and lexemes are native, but the grammatical usage seems to be borrowed. Among Mayan languages, noun classifiers are basically limited to the languages of the Cuchumatanes (Chujean, Kanjobalan, and some Mam), but see Grinevald Craig (1990) for a broader view. Colonial data suggest numeral classifiers may have occurred in other languages as well but have since disappeared.

Onomatopoetic roots (ONOM) constitute a small class of roots that appear to result from onomatopoeia, including the imitation of sounds from inanimate sources, animal cries, calls to animals, and exclamations: *pem*, bang!; *tit*, the sound of a car horn; *ch'op*, the sound of a stick being pulled out of the mud; *ch'ek*, the call of a grackle; *pix*, call to a dog; *ay*, exclamation of pain, *hi'*, affirmative response; *hay*, hailing call.

Particle roots (PAR) are distinguished from all other classes by the lack of derivation to form verbs, nouns, or other stem classes. Native particles are of the shape CVC, but there are many particles introduced from Spanish that have varied shapes. Some particles and particle clusters occur as modifiers of verb phrases. The most common particle, marked below as locative (LOC) is *t'a(y)*, "in, at, to, from, with"; this sole preposition introduces oblique phrases in verbal constructions (locatives, instrumentals, and so forth, but not subject or object).

Inflectional Morphology

Chuj has an impressive inventory of pre-and post-fixed inflectional and deriva-tional morphemes. They can be divided into three overlapping sets based on the na-ture of the roots and stems to which they are attached: intransitive, transitive, and positional verbs. The latter resemble in their inflection the single existential verb.

Following general Mayanist usage, pronominal affixes for subjects and objects are labeled here by numbers for persons (1, 2 and 3 = first, second and third per-son; sg = singular; pl = plural; note that 3sg = 3pl, and may be marked simply 3).

The two sets of pronominal markers are designated by letters: Set A = subjects of transitive verbs (VTR) and possessors of nouns; Set B = subjects of intransitive verbs (VIN) and objects of VTR. Thus, A1sg is first person singular "I" (as subject of VTR); B1sg is "I" (as subject of VIN), "me" (as object of VTR), and "my" (as possessor of nouns).

In general, the inflectional prefixes are as follows (in sets according to their relative distance from the following or preceding stem):

-9   negative (NEG): *ma-*
      (combines with-8/-7 to form *ma-j-, ma-x-, ma-nh-'ol, ma-nh-wan-ok-laj, ma-x-wal, ma-nh, ma-j*)

-8   tense-aspect (CP, ICP, DUR): *ix-, ts-, x-, ø-, j-, nh-*
      past completive, present incompletive, durative, punctual, negative past durative, negative future or progressive durative

-7   tense-aspect (FUT, PROG): *ol, wal, wan(-ok-laj)*
      future inchoative, progressive, progressive (requires VTR-*an-(ih)* inflection)

-6   state of knowledge (INT, REP): *ham-, hab'-*
      interrogative, reportative

-5   directional motion (DIR):-*ek',-em,-el, uch,-kan,-kut,-b'at,-k'e',-k'och,-hul,-xit'*
      pass by, go down, leave, enter, remain, draw near, go, rise, arrive, come, go and return

-4   object: *hin-, hach-, ø-, honh-, hex-*
      (A1SG, A2SG, A3, A1PL, A2PL)

-3   directional motion (DIR): *ek'-*(and possibly others)
      See +5

-2   subject: *hin-, hach-, ø-, honh-, hex-; ha-, s-, ko-, he-; w-, h-, y-, k-, hey-*
      (A1SG/B1SG, A2SG, A3, A1PL, A2PL; B2SG, B3, B1PL, B2PL; B1SG, B2SG, B3, B1PL, B2PL)

-1   intensive (INTS): *te-*

Verbal suffixes include the following (in sets according to their relative distance from the stem):

+1   state of knowledge:-*tah,-ok*; clitics-*hV' ~-'Vh,-(ih)*
      uncertainty, doubt (IRR); phrase-final VTR (TV) and VIN (ITV) clitics

+2   imperative (IMP):-*anh*
      for VIN, replaces-*(ih)*; for VTR clitics are retained without this suffix

+3   plural of imperative:-*ek*
      for VIN, replaces-*(ih)*; for VTR, replaces clitics

+4   repetition (REPET):-*(i)x,-pax*
      single repetition of action

+5   directional motion (unstressed) (DIR):-*ek',-em,-el,-uch,-kan,-kut,-b'at,-k'e',-k'och,-hul*

      pass by, go down, leave, enter, remain, draw near, go, rise, arrive, come

+6   directional motion (stressed)(DIR): *'ék', 'ém, 'él, 'óch, kán, kót, b'át, k'é, k'óch, húl*

      pass by, go down, leave, enter, remain, draw near, go, rise, arrive, come

+7   motion toward speaker:-*tah*
      (occurs only with verbs of directional motion, including +5/+6)

+8   negative (NEG):-*laj*
      (occurs only after-*ma* in-9)

+9   plural of third person (3PL):-*heb'*
      (non-obligatory; occurs only with third person A3/ B3 subjects/objects)

+10   clitic (ITV):-*(ih)*
      (with VIN only, and only if phrase-final; does not occur if +7/+8/+9
      is filled)

The inventory of affixes surrounding stative stems is more limited than
the above, but the meanings and functions are the same for corresponding
morphemes:

-3   negative: *ma-*
-2   intensive: *te-*
-1   possessor: *hin-, ha-, s-, ko-, he-, w-, h-, y-, k-, hey-*
ø   root or stem
+1   extended action or existence:-*an*
+2   subject:-*in,-ach,-ø,-onh,-ex*
      A1, A2, A3/6, A4, A5
3   state of knowledge:-*ham,-hab'*
+4   repetition: *páx*
+5   directional motion:-*ek',-em,-el,-uch,-kan,-kut,-b'at,-k'e',-k'och,-hul*
+6   directional motion: *'ék', 'ém, 'él, 'óch, kán, kót, b'át, k'é, k'óch, húl*
+7   negative:-*laj*
+8   plural of third person:-*heb'*
+9   clitic:-*(ih)*

The stems that are inflected by the affixes listed above come from verb, noun, positional, and onomatopoetic roots. Verb roots may be transitive (VTR), intransitive (VIN), positional (VPO), or existential (VEX) verbs. Noun roots include substantive (N), adjective (ADJ), numeral (NUM) and noun classifier (NCLF) nouns. Positional roots may be distributive or nondistributive. There is only one existential root, *ay* "to be."

Affixes of directional motion are very common. In general, the prefixed affixes of directional motion modify the action of the subject (that is, to do something *while passing by*). The set of directional motion suffixes closest to the stem modify the action itself (that is, to do something *in a lateral motion*), and those more distant relate to the movements of the actor (*while moving sideways*).

The Formation of Stems from Verbal Roots

The derivation of roots to form stems of various classes is accomplished through suffixation of single suffixes or desinences (common combinations of suffixes). The classification of the resulting forms is based on their inflectional characteristics (see above).

(1) Transitive Verb Stems Derived from Transitive Verb Roots. The following suffixes and desinences (DER) derive transitive verb stems from transitive roots:

-ej	forms transitive verb stems from derived transitive stems, but also from nontransitive roots, including noun roots and stems.
-w-ej	forms transitive verbs from transitive verb roots.
-ch-it-ej	forms transitive verbs of complete action. Passives are formed by *–ch-it-aj-(ih)*.
	Nouns may be formed by *–ch-im-tak*.
-ts-it-ej	forms transitive verbs of repetitive action.
-l-it-ej	forms transitive verbs that express causative action. Passives are formed by *–l-aj-(ih);-l-an-(ih)* also forms apparent passives.
-m-it-ej	forms transitive verbs of related meaning. Passives are formed by *–m-aj-(ih)*.

(2) Intransitive Verb Stems Derived from Transitive Verb Roots:

-w-(ih)	forms intransitive verb stems from transitive verb roots.
-b'-an-(ih)	forms intransitive verb stems from transitive verb roots.

-aj-(ih)	forms intransitive (passive) verb stems from transitive verb stems formed with *(i)t-,-ch-,-k'-,-m-,-n-,-w-*, and *–l-*.
-ax-(ih)	forms intransitive (passive) stems from transitive verb roots.
-n-ax-(ih)	forms intransitive (passive) verbs from transitive verb roots.

(3) Nouns Derived from Transitive Verb Roots:

-ab'-(il)	forms nouns referring to people or things that perform the transitive action or that are its object. These suffixes may follow other derivations.
-ub'	forms nouns referring to objects that result from the action of the verb.
-um	forms agentive nouns, referring to people or things that accomplish the action of the verb.
-nak	forms nouns referring to persons or things that have performed the verbal action. This suffix more commonly occurs on intransitive stems.
-oj	forms nouns that refer to acts.
-al and *–ul*	form nouns that refer to the results of actions.
-il	forms nouns that refer to instruments that carry out the verbal action.
-em	forms nouns (participles) that refer to objects of the verbal action.
-b'-il	forms nouns (participles) that refer to objects of the verb.
-b'-en	forms nouns that refer to the objects of the verb.

(4) There are very few derivations formed from intransitive verb roots. Many of these forms suggest bivalence of the verb root VIN/VTR, since the derivations are found in transitive verb derivations. Known examples include the following:

-ch-it-aj-(ih)	forms intransitive verbs indicating completeness of action. (see VTR-*ch-it-ej* and VTR-*ch-it-aj-(ih)*, transitive verb and its passive, above).
-um	forms agentive nouns. Note that this form implies bivalence of the root (see VTR-*um* nouns, above).
-el	forms nouns referring to acts or results of the intransitive action.

Stems Derived from Positional Verb Roots. Unlike the members of other verb classes, positional verb roots never occur underived. Perhaps as a consequence, there are more derivational suffixes and desinences for the derivation of positional verb roots than there are for any other verb class.

(5) Transitive Verb Stems Derived from Positional Verb Roots (note that all are causative in meaning):

-b'-it-ej	forms transitive (causative) verb stems from transitive verb roots.
-ub'-tanh-ej	forms transitive (causative) verb stems from transitive verb roots.
-l-aj-cham-b'ah	forms transitive (causative) verb stems from transitive verb roots.

(6) Intransitive Verb Stems Derived from Positional Verb Roots. Note that the majority refer to displaying or taking on the characteristics indicated by the positional verb root. Many involve some form of reduplication, partial or complete, a common feature of positional verbs in Mayan languages.

-k-ih	derives a single intransitive verb stem: *tak-k-ih*, to dry out.
-b'-(ih)	forms intransitive verb stems meaning to take on the features of the VPO; further derivation of VIN is with *–b'-an-(ih)*. Nouns are formed with *–b'-al*.
-w-ih	*forms intransitive verb stems meaning to express the features of the VPO. Nouns are formed with –w-al.*
-k'-aj-(ih)	forms intransitive verb stems meaning to display the features of the VPO. Similar verbs are formed with *–an-k'-aj-(ih)*.
-n-aj-(ih)	forms intransitive verb stems meaning to display the features of the VPO. Corresponding adverbs are derived by *–n-aj-ok*.
-Vl-j-(ih)	forms intransitive verb stems meaning to express the features of the VPO. Corresponding adverbs are formed by *–Vl-j-ok*.
-Vl-j-ub'-(ih)	forms intransitive verb stems meaning to display the features of the VPO.
-C$_i$-on-(ih)	derives intransitive verb stems meaning to display the features of the VPO. Corresponding adverbs are formed with *–C1-on-ok*.
-VC$_2$-(ih)	forms intransitive verb stems. Corresponding adverbs are formed with *–VC$_2$-ok*.
-CVC-an-(ih)	forms intransitive verb stems (complete reduplication of the VPO root). Corresponding adverbs are derived in *–CVC-an-ok*.

(7) Nouns Derived from Positional Verb Roots:

-b'-ab'-(il)	derives noun stems meaning things that have the features of the VPO root.
-il-tak	derives noun stems meaning things that display the features of the VPO.
-C_i-um-b'ah	derives nouns meaning things that display the features of the VPO root.
-(k')-ech-tak	derives noun stems meaning things that have the features of the VPO; the suffix *tak* (plurality, multiplicity) is obligatory.
-u'-(Noun)	derives noun stems; other than *pek-u'*, "chicken with short legs" <VPO *pek*, "low to the ground," known examples form compound noun stems, that is, *punh-u'-jolom,* "round-headed person" <VPO /punh/ "small and spherical."
-i-CVC	derives one known noun, *sur-i-sur*, "whirligig" <VPO *xi*, "whirling around."
-inh	derives one known noun stem, adj *tak-inh*, "dry" <VPO *tak*, "dry."

(8) Other Stems Derived from Positional Verb Roots:

-inh	One example only: *tak-inh*, "dry," adjective. See *tak-k-ih*, "to dry out," above.
-an	derives stative stems from positional verb roots.
-anh	derives numeral classifier stems from positional verb roots.

(9) Verbal Stems Derived from Noun Roots:

-ej	derives active transitive verb stems from noun stems.
-t-ej	derives active transitive verb stems from noun stems. Passives are formed with *–t-aj-(ih).*

Compound Verb Stems

Several types of verb stems include more than one root. The verbs of directional motion, treated here as verbal inflection, could be considered parts of compound verbs, but the changes in meaning caused by their use are minor. Four other kinds of compound verbs have been noted. One is causative, one incorporates

Spanish infinitives into the verbal system; another incorporates noun stems into the verbal construction. A final type, not fully understood because of its syntactic peculiarities, is based on verbs of directional motion and incorporates adverbial stems into the compound verb.

Causative compound verb stems are based on the transitive verb *ak'*, to do something. Following the transitive root is an intransitive verb stem with various suffixes. The suffix *-an* indicates on-going action. The desinence on the main (first) verb *-n-aj-(ih)/* forms passive constructions, and the suffix *-ok* may occur in place of *-(ih): ak'-jenhwok*, "to cause something to fly" (<*jenh-w-(ih)*, "to fly"); *ak'-k'ewanok*, "to cause something to rise" (<*k'e'-w-(ih)*, "to rise"); *ak'naj-achan-wok*, to be caused to bathe (<*ach-an-w-(ih)*, "to bathe").

Spanish infinitives are incorporated into the verb stem by suffixing them to the verb stem *ak'(an): ak'an-despedir*, "to say goodbye"; *ak'an-ganar*, "to earn something"; *ak'an-konsegir*, "to acquire something." The set of incorporated Spanish verbs is probably an open set.

The third type of compound verb stem incorporates noun objects into the verb stem; the transitive verb root is suffixed with *-w-(ih)* to form an intransitive stem, and the following noun is obligatorily unstressed and cannot be inflected: *páywih-nhal*, to dry maize by heating (<VTR *pay-ej*, "to dry something by heating"; and N *nhal*, "maize ear"); *áwwih-'awal*, "to plant maize" (<VTR *aw*, "to plant something," and N *awal*, "cornfield").

The final type of compound verb stem has syntactic complications. The compounds are usually based on a verb of directional motion, and the second component is an intransitive verb stem derived by a number of suffixes. The complications—too complex to be discussed here— arise in that the second element may occur in front of the main verb as well as suffixed, and the inflectional patterns vary from transitive to intransitive. For a discussion, see Hopkins (1970b).

Compound Noun Stems

Three types of compound noun stems are formed by the combination of (1) a substantive, adjective, numeral or noun classifier root with a following substantive noun; (2) a positional or transitive verb root with a following substantive noun; and (3) two or more numeral roots and stems. Two attested stems appear to combine numeral and positional roots to form a compound verb stem. Conklin (1962:122–23) suggested that compounds can be divided into unitary and composite lexemes: "unitary lexemes ... no segments of which may designate categories which are identical to, or subordinate to, those designated by the forms in question"; and "composite lexemes . . . one or more segments of which, under specified conditions, may (a) designate the same categories as those designated by the forms in question (abbreviation), or (b) designate categories superordinate to those designated by the forms in question (generalization)." Unitary lexemes are either simple (unsegmentable) or complex (segmentable).

Substantive noun plus substantive noun compounds can be either head-initial composite lexemes, attribute-initial composite lexemes, or complex unitary lexemes. Head-initial composite lexemes include *ti'-k'u'*, "blanket hole" (<"edge/lip" and "blanket"), *stsa'-taj*, "pine sap" (<"excrement" and "pine"), *mak'lab'-much*, "pole used for striking down birds" (<"something used for striking" and "bird"). Attribute-initial composite lexemes include *ts'um-k'e'en*, "sheet tin" (<"leather/hide" and "stone/metal"), *ch'ow-kuuk*, "a kind of squirrel" (<"rat" and "squirrel"), *chej-chan*, "a mythical snake" (<"deer" and "snake"). Complex unitary lexemes include *tanh-patik*, "poor person" (<"ash" and "back"). *chich-ti'*, "hare-lipped person" (<"hare" and "lip"), *k'uxum-woton*, "weasel" (<"eater" and "button"), *t'oyum-'une'*, "oppossum" (<"carrier of something in a pocket," and "child").

Adjective noun plus substantive noun compounds are attribute-initial composite lexemes: *tul-kamix,* "short shirt" (<"short" and "shirt"), *chak-choj,/* "mountain lion" (<"red" and "puma"), *nit-k'anal,* "Venus" (<"large" and "star").

Numeral noun plus substantive noun compounds are rare, and their types are mixed: *cha'-jaj,* "trachea" (<"two" and "throat"), *ho'-k'ante',* "the place name Ocanté" (<"five" and "birch tree"), *jun-'ix,* widow (<"one" and "woman").

Noun classifier plus substantive noun compounds appear to be fossilized phrases; stress on the noun classifiers varies (although they are unstressed when functioning as demonstratives): *k'ina-nhab',* "rain" (<"rain classifier" and "rain"), *anh-k'ultak,* "brushland" (<"herbaceous plant classifier" and "brushland").

Positional root plus substantive noun compounds are attribute-initial composite and unitary complex lexemes: *konh-te',* "arch" or "bow" (<"arched" and "wood"), *ij-te',* prop (<"leaning against something" and "wood"), *t'en-ti',* "hairless lip or chin" (<"bare" and "mouth/lip"), *b'el-jom,* "a type of large gourd" (<"split lengthwise" and "gourd bowl"); *b'ik-nhej,* "oppossum" (<"too thin for its length" and "tail"), *b'ech-k'ab',* "hand wave" (<"overhanging" and "hand"); *t'en-jolom,* "bald person" (<"bare" and "head").

Transitive verb plus substantive noun compounds are unitary composite lexemes: *kol-k'ab',* "ring (jewelry)" (<"defend" and "hand"), *ch'iy-'eh,* "canine tooth" (<"rip into strips" and "tooth"), *jal-te',* "cage" (<"weave" and "wood"), *nits-k'uh,* "plant name" (<"move something" and "sun").

Numeral plus numeral noun compounds form numeral stems whose value is greater than twelve; *ox-lajunh*, "thirteen" (<"three" and "ten"), *b'alunh-lajunh*, "nineteen" (<"nine" and "ten"), *jun-winak*, "twenty" (<"one" and "score"), *cha'-winak*, "forty" ("two" and "score"), *jun-k'al*, "four hundred" ("one" and "four hundred"). A few compounds formed by complete or partial reduplication and found only in words relating to the passage of time are *chab'-chab'*, "every two" ("every other one" <"two" and "two"), as in *xch'ab'chab' k'uhal*, "every other day"; *s-laj-lajunh-ej-ih-al*, "every ten days" (<"ten").

Numeral noun plus numeral classifier compounds are rare; only two examples are known. The first is *ox-t'ilanh*, "the three stars of Orion's belt" (<"three" and numeral classifier *t'il-anh*), but *t'il* refers to "lines of things," not "things in a line." It is possible that this is a fossilized compound that originally referred to the triangle formed by one waist star and two knee stars, since this constellation is recognized in Classic Maya epigraphy as the First Hearth, three stones with a fire (the Orion Nebula) inside the triangle; the three-stone hearth is a Mesoamerican culture trait. The shift to Orion's belt may be influenced by the corresponding Spanish constellation, The Three Marys (*las tres Marías*), sometimes The Three Kings (*los tres reyes*). The second compound is *jun-kot*, "*andasolo*, a solitary male coatí" (younger males are gregarious, older males solitary) (<"one" and the numeral classifier for "standing on four legs").

Phrase Structure

The syntax of Chuj sentences involves four kinds of phrases: verb, stative, particle, and noun phrases. The first three are relatively simple, but noun phrases are very complex. The verb phrase consists of an inflected verb stem; minimal inflection is for personal subject. All other inflection is optional. If a verb is inflected for anything other than subject, it is inflected for tense/aspect. The stative phrase consists of an inflected stative stem. Like the verb phrase, minimal inflection is for subject, and all other inflection is optional, except that stative phrases are not inflected for tense/aspect. The nucleus of a stative phrase is often a substantive or adjectival noun phrase recruited to act as predicate. Particle phrases consist of clusters of particles that have no head-attribute structure; they are difficult to gloss in isolation, just as individual particles are difficult to gloss: *hanheja'*, (*ha'-nhej-ha'*), "just like that"; *tatoh* (*tah-toh*), "still" or "yet"; *matoh* (*ma'-toh*), "but if." These phrases often introduce noun or verb phrases, but are not the heads of the noun or verb phrase.

Noun phrases consist minimally in an uninflected noun stem, which may in turn be an underived noun root. The maximum complexity of noun phrases involves embedded sentences that function as nouns. Other than simple nouns, in terms of their composition there are at least seven types of noun phrases, as follows.

Noun classifier phrases consist of a noun classifier and its associated noun or noun phrase, which may be an embedded sentence. The noun classifier in these constructions remains unstressed (as opposed to the stressed forms serving as pronouns): *nok' chítam*, "the (animal class) pig"; *heb' nok' hin chítam*, "my (animal class) pigs"; *nok' sts'úmal sk'én winh yúk'tak smám wính*, "the (animal class [leather]) scabbard of the knife of his father's brother" (enclosing the noun classifier phrase *winh yúk'tak smám wính*, "his father's brother"); *winh smúnlaj t'a sk'éxan k'áb'*, "a (human class) man who works with his left hand."

Possessive noun phrases consist of the possessed noun and its possessor: *sjolom spenek winh*, "the head of his knee"; *syempuhal kak'an'och kawal*, "the time we work in the cornfield."

Two types of enumerative noun phrases involve numeral roots and stems. The first is composed of a numeral root or compound numeral stem and a numeral classifier stem. The numerical part may be suffixed with *-tak* distributive, or followed by an adjective, that is, *kotak*, "small," *niwan*, "large (singular)," or *niwak*, "large (plural)": *wak b'ech*, "six handfuls"; *waktak b'ech*, "six handfuls each"; *cha' kotak patsanh*, "two small fiber bundles"; *jun niwan patsanh*, "one large fiber bundle." The second type of enumerative noun phrases is composed of a noun stem derived from a numeral root by the derivation *-e'*, and a following noun referring to a set of measures; these constructions may be suffixed by *-ok*, "approximately," or with particles, especially *nhej*, "only," *toh*, "still": *wake' kintal*, "six hundredweights" (<Spanish *quintal*); *wake'ok kintal*, "about six hundredweights"; *oxe nhej b'arah*, "only three varas (a Spanish measure of about thirty-three inches)."

Quantitative noun phrases consist of one of the preceding enumerative noun phrases and a following noun that expresses what is being quantified: *wake kintal tut*, "six quintales of beans"; *waktak b'ech anh stut heb' winh*, "six handsful each of their (plant class) beans"; *wak wanh winh smunlaj t'ah sk'exan k'ab'*, "six (human class) men who work with their left hands."

Demonstrative noun phrases consist of a noun phrase, usually a noun classifier phrase, followed by either of the adjectival nouns *chi'*, "there" or *tik*, "here," indicating relative proximity: *winh chi'*, that man; *heb' ix ix tik*, "these women"; *ixim wawal tik*, "this cornfield of mine"; *heb' winh slechank'eta chi'*, "those men who dip out [the salt water]."

Any noun phrase other than embedded sentences may be preceded or followed, or both, by particles, to form a particle noun phrase. Particles commonly preceding noun phrases are *ha'*, "demonstrative"; *t'ah ~ t'ay*, "locative or oblique"; *te*, "intensive," and *mas*, "comparative." Common postposed particles are *xoh*, "already," *toh*, "still," and *nhej*, "only": *ha ta'*, "in that place"; *t'a pinkah*, "in/at/to/ from the plantations"; *t'a jun xoh k'uhtik*, "today (on this other day)"; *mas wach'*, "better (more good)"; *wach' xoh*, "already well"; *te pural*, "with much difficulty," *ich nhej ta'*, "in this way alone."

Embedded sentence noun phrases differ from independent sentences only in simplicity; they are not preceded by particle phrases or conjunctions, but begin with the topic phrase or a later phrase (see below). The independent sentence *smunlaj winh anima t'a swach' k'ab'*, "the man works with his right hand," will appear as an embedded sentence as *winh anima smunlaj t'a swach' k'ab'*, "the man who works with his right hand." Embedded sentences may occur in any of the noun phrase positions of the sentence (topics, preposed adverbials, direct objects, subjects, or post-posed adverbials). Examples are (embedded sentences in brackets): *ha xo winh [ayem k'och chi'], xcha'an lu'um*, "the other man [(who) is down there on top] receives the earthen pot"; *ha [skomunlajih], skoman ket'b'eyum*, "when[we work], we hire our helpers"; *yah [hin xit'ek'] yuj nhab' t'a ketsal*, "painful was [my trip (I went and returned)] because of the rain at Quetzal"; *ay b'aj [smunlaj winh]*, "there is a place where [he works]"; *ixin na'elta [ixin b'at t'a wariyah]*, "I thought about [going to Barillas (I went to Barillas)]."

Sentence Structure

The Basic Word Order of a Chuj sentence is VOS, a Main phrase (Verb or stative) followed by Noun phrases representing the Object (if the verb is transitive) and Subject of the sentence. This cluster of phrases may be preceded and/ or followed by Adverbial phrases. Either of the Object and Subject Phrases can be fronted to a Topic phrase position before the Adverbial Phrase (often leaving a noun classifier in the post-verbal position). Finally, this complex of phrases may be preceded by an Introductory phrase and/or followed by a Clitic phrase. The complete set of phrases as sentence elements is thus: Introductory, Topic, Adverbial, Main, Object, Subject, Adverbial, and Clitic.

The Introductory phrase position is filled by particle and noun phrases, including a large number of items borrowed from Spanish. This position functions to link sentences, that is, it serves as a sentence conjunction. Loan words include *peroh*, "but"; *porke*, "because"; *por esoh*, "for this reason"; *keh*, a subordinating conjunction (from Spanish *que*); *komoh*, "as, since"; *ih*, "and"; *entonseh*, "then"; *yakeh*, "since, while," and *bwenoh*, "well." Native items include *tah (toh)*, "if"; *xal*, "and";

hok xoh, "but, or"; *ma toh*, "but, or"; *waya'*, "also"; *wach' chom*, "even though"; *yos*, "and," and especially in narratives, *yuj chi'*, "for that reason": *[yuj chi'], ha' tsonh munlajih, skoman ket'b'eyum, skoman ket'b'eyum*, "[for that reason], when we work, we hire helpers."

The Topic phrase position is filled by a noun phrase, the topicalization of the post-verbal Subject or Object phrase. Two Topic phrases that do not have the same referent may co-occur, for example, an indirect and direct object: *[ha' heb' winh slechank'etah], [jun sentawuh] skotup jun jun ch'ub'*, "To [those men who dip out (the salt)], [one cent] we pay them, for each pot."

The preposed Adverbial phrase is filled by one or more particle or noun phrases, the latter usually an embedded sentence or a locative phrase introduced by *t'ah ~ t'ay*. Examples are: *entonseh [mas nhej] sb'at t'ah yib'anh*, "then [even more] it comes down on us"; *ha' [t'ah spatik lum pinkah], ha' ta' ix pitzwih winh*, "There [in plantation country], there he grew up."

The Main phrase position is filled by a verb or stative phrase. Stative phrases are noun phrases (including adjectival phrases) that have been recruited as predicates, taking the place of a verb: *[te niwak] lum ch'ub'*, "[Very heavy] (are) the pots"; *[nab'a ha'] atz'am*, "[Pure liquid] (is) the salt"; *[ladinu] heb' winh chi'*, "[Ladinos] those men (are)."

The Object phrase position, which occurs only if a transitive verb phrase fills the Main phrase position, is filled by one or more Noun phrases that agree in person with the pronominal object of the verb; the Noun phrase may be an embedded sentence: *skuchan [lum] heb' winh*, "The men carry [the (earthen) pot]"; *ol ko t'okank'e [lum ko lu'um]*, "We will turn [our land]"; *ol wala' [chajtil skutej sk'etah atz'am atz'am]*, "I will talk about [how we bring out the salt]."

The Subject phrase position is filled by a Noun phrase that agrees in person with the pronominal subject of the Main phrase. If the detailed Subject noun phrase has been fronted to Topic, the Subject phrase position may be filled by a pronoun or the corresponding noun classifier: *[ha heb' winh t'unhum ch'ub' chi'], chekel nhej [heb' winh]* "[Those men who carry the pots], chosen (are) [they]"; *[ha ha ha'], seb'nhej ko k'echan chanh ha'*, "[That water], easily we can lift [it]."

The post-posed Adverbial phrase position is filled by one or more Noun phrases. Combinations of time and place, or two adverbials of place, have been observed. Phrases in this oblique phrase position are often introduced by *t'ah ~ t'ay*, "at, in, on," etc.; *et'*, "with," or other subordinating phrases: *syamchaj nok' [ku'uj]*, "The animals are caught [by us]"; *ix yak'an despedir winh [t'ay hin]*, "He said goodbye [to me]"; *sb'at winh [chonhab']*, "He goes [to town]."

The Clitic phrase position is filled by *b'i' ~ b'ihan*, which only occurs if the sentence is terminal, that is, if it is not an embedded sentence or is not followed by another sentence linked by a conjunction. In conversation *b'i'* functions like a sentence tag, similar to English "Okay?," a request for affirmation: *hin b'at het', b'i',* "I'm going with you, okay?" In narrations, a gloss of "so" is perhaps appropriate: *yos, ol ko tsikanpax lum, och ixim kawal, b'ihan,* "And, we turn the earth again, our cornfield comes in, so"; *t'ah jun k'uh, skotsol k'ak' t'ah sti'tak lum, cha'an sk'ak'al lum, stsab'at lum, b'ihan,* "The next day, we set fire to the edges of the field, so the land catches fire, it burns up, so."

A second phrase final clitic, *jun,* may occur at the end of any phrase but is most frequent at the end of embedded sentences that are linked to a following sentence by conjunctions: *xal tah ma'ay [jun], skona'eltah,* "And if it is not, [well], we think about it"; *eh, tato te k'en lum[jun], sk'enal sat lum, max yallaj ko pilan yip,* "And if the earth is very rocky, [well], (if) its surface is rocky, we can't make haste."

Coyote and Rabbit

The following presentation of the Coyote-Rabbit story shows the text in a multi-line format that records the text in a modern orthographic (line 1) and technical morphophonemic (line 2) transcription, morpheme-by-morpheme breakdown (line 3) with identification of the morphemes (line 4), followed by sentence structures (line 5) and phrase-by-phrase English gloss (line 6). Internal phrase structure is indicated by hash marks (#), and these correspond in lines 2–6. To the right of the text are marginal notes labeling gross discourse sections of the text. Note that lines 2 and 3 revert to a morphophonemic transcription in which glottal stop is recorded in all positions (as <7>), and *ts* and *ts'* are transcribed <tz, tz'> to demonstrate they are unitary phonemes, not combinations of two consonants, *t* and *s*, following Kaufman (2003). Line 2 also marks stress patterns.

Individual morphemes are identified using the abbreviations of Aissen et al. (2017:vii–xx) and Mateo Toledo (2017) except that I have merged abbreviations to form NCLF (noun classifier) and NUMCLF (numeral classifier). In the conventions of this marking, major roots such as nouns and verbs are not marked as such but are translated, that is, *jun okes chi'*, NUM coyote DEM, "that coyote." Root classes can be inferred from the kinds of affixes taken by these roots and stems. Morpheme identifiers used in this text are displayed in the following chart (chart 2). Many of the derivational affixes are marked only as DER; these can be found in the grammar sketch, above.

This transcription covers only the first of several episodes of the narrative as told by the narrator; following episodes (not shown, but included in the AILLA archive recording) have the same overall structure. The text begins with a brief opening and evidentiality statement: there is a story, and it comes from our ancestors in the distant past.

The first episode follows the introductory remarks. It consists of three extended events. In a theatrical production, an episode would be presented as an act, a set of related actions telling a coherent part of the overall story. Each event within an episode would constitute a scene, as the setting and/or protagonists change from one to another. Here, the first event introduces Coyote and a peripheral figure, an old Ram. The scene changes, and the second event features the interaction

CHART 2. Abbreviations

Pronouns

A1SG, A2SG, A3, A1PL, A2PL, first through third person singular and plural, Set A (ergative pronouns); B1SG, B2SG, B3, B1PL, B2PL, first through third person singular and plural, Set B (absolutive pronouns). A3 and B3 are ambiguous for number.

Roots and Stems

ADV, adverbial; CL, clitic; DEM, demonstrative; EXCLAM, exclamatory; EXH, exhortative; LOC, locative; NCLF, noun classifier NUM, numeral; NUMCLF, numeral classifier; PAR, particle; Q, interrogative. Nouns, verbs, and other major classes are translated rather than classified.

Affixes

BEN, benefactive; CAUS, causative; CP, completive aspect; DIR, directional; DUB, dubitative; DUR, durative aspect; FUT, future aspect; ICP, incompletive aspect; IMP, imperative; IRR, irrealis; ITV, intransitive verb suffix; NEG, negative; PROG, progressive aspect; PSV, passive; PTCP, participle; REP, reportative; TV, transitive verb suffix. DER marks unspecified derivation.

---

between Coyote and Rabbit. Without a change in setting but sometime later, the final event involves only Coyote. Each event begins with background information and proceeds to dialogue; the peak of each event is related as a conversation. The events end with closings. The final event, Coyote's soliloquy, is marked as the peak of this episode by the parallelisms of the monologue: a couplet and a triplet.

Each of the following episodes (not shown here) has the same structure: Coyote comes upon Rabbit in a new setting, introducing a new topic (the mist-covered rock, the potato, the tar baby, and so forth). Events are related in dialogue, and each episode closes with Coyote, having been tricked again, swearing vengeance on Rabbit as he leaves to go look for him.

Text Analysis

[Discourse Notes in Brackets]
Chuj Text in Modern Orthography
Morphophonemic Transcription (unintended text in parentheses)
Morpheme (-) and Phrase (#) Boundaries
Morpheme Identification
Identification of Phrases
Phrase-by-Phrase English Gloss

*

[Opening]

Chitik ha wal jun yik'ti'al yaj.

Chí tik (tik) há wal jun yík'ti7al yáj.

chi7 tik # ha7 wal jun y-7ík'-ti7-al # y-7áj

DEM DEM # DEM PROG NUM A3SG-story # A3SG-be

Intro # Topic # Main Phrase

Well # there is a story # that exists

[Evidentiality Statement]

Ay wal jun yik'ti' ko mam kicham chi' ay kani.

7áy wal jun yík'ti7 ko mám kícham chí7 7áy kaníh.

7ay-Ø wal # jun y-7ik-ti7 ko-mam k-7icham chi7 [#] 7ay-Ø-kan-ih

exist-B3SG PROG # NUM A3SG-story A1PL-grandfather-A1PLU-uncle DEM

   [#] stay-DIR-ITV

Main Phrase # Subject

There is # a story of our ancestors which remains

Hab' yak' jun tsanh ko mam kicham chi', peka'.

Hap' yák' jun tzanh ko mám kícham chi7, péká7.

hap'-Ø-y-7ak' # jun-tzanh ko-mam k-7icham chi7 # pek-a7

REP-B3-A3-do # NUM-NUMCLF A1PL-grandfather A1PL-uncle DEM

   # past-DER

Main Phrase # Subject # Adverbial

they say they did it # some of our ancestors # in the past

[First Event]

[Background]

Ayab' nok' ch'ak kalnel.

7áyap' nok' ch'ák kálnel.

7ay-Ø-hap' # nok' ch'ak kalnel

exist-B3-REP # NCLF horn goat

Main Phrase # Subject

they say there was # a male sheep

Ay wanok mam ch'ak kalnel.

7áy wanok mám ch'ák kálnel.

7ay-Ø wan-ok # mam ch'ak kalnel

exist-B3 PROG-IRR # grandfather horn goat

Main Phrase # Subject

there was # an old male sheep

Xch'okoj nok' sb'ey t'a jun b'e chi'.

Xch'ókoj nok' sp'éy t'a jun p'éh chí7.

s-ch'ok-oj nok' # tz-Ø-p'ey # t'ah jun p'eh chi7

A3-alone-DER NCLF # ICP-B3-walk # LOC NUM road DEM

Topic # Main Phrase # Adverbial

the animal alone # walks # on a road there

Cha'an'el sb'a nok' ch'ak kalnel chi'. . . jun okes.

Cháan 7el sp'áh nok' ch'ák kálnel chí7 (jun jun jun) jun 7ókés.

cha7-an-Ø-el # s-p'ah # nok' ch'ak kalnel chi7 # jun 7okes

find-PTCP-B3-DIR # A3-self # NCLF horn sheep DEM # NUM coyote

Main Phrase # Object # Subject # Subject

met # themselves # that male sheep # [and] a coyote

Antonse t'a yem xo k'uhalil cha'anab' el sb'a jun okes chi' yet' jun ch'ak
   kalnel chi'.

7antónse t'ah yém xoh k'úhalil cháanap' 7él sp'áh jun 7ókes chi7 yet' jun
   ch'ák kálnel chí7.

7antonse # t'ah y-7em xoh k'uh-al-il # cha7-an-Ø-hap'-7el # s-p'ah # jun
   7okes chi7 y-7et' jun ch'ak kalnel chi7

then # LOC A3-fall ADV sun-DER-DER # find-PTCP-B3-REP-DIR # A3-self #
   NUM coyote DEM A#-accompany NUM horn sheep DEM

Intro # Adverbial # Main Phrase # Object # Subject

then # when the sun was already low # they say were found # themselves #
   that Coyote and the Ram

Xal tik ne'ik.

Xál tik néik.

xal tik ne7ik

ADV ADV ADV-DER

Intro [Adverbial Clause]:

Here now:

[Dialogue]

"Ke, ch'ak kalnel.

"Keh, ch'ák kálnel.

keh # ch'ak kalnel

EXH # horn sheep

Topic # Topic

"You # Ram

To tsin k'anb'ej t'ayach.
To tzin k'ánp'ej t'áyach,
toh # tz-Ø-hin-k'an-p'-ej # t'ay-hach
still # ICP-B3-A1SG-ask-BEN-TV # LOC-B2SG
Adverbial # Main Phrase # Adverbial
still # I ask # to you

¿Mama b'aj ix hil winh wamigu, winh konejo?
máma p'áj ʔix híl winh wámigu, (winh) winh kónejoh.
ma-ham haʔ-Ø # p'aj ʔix-Ø-h-ʔil winh w-ʔamiguh winh konejoh
NEG-IRR DEM-B3 # where ICP-B3-A2SG-see A1SG-friend NCLF rabbit
Main Phrase # Subject
isn't there # where you saw my friend the Rabbit

To ay janik' junin tarate yet' winh.
To ʔáy jánik' junin táráte yét' wính.
toh # ʔay-Ø jan-ik' # jun hin-tarateh y-ʔet' winh
Adverbial # exist-B3 Q-DER # NUM A1SG-date A3-accompany NCLF
Adverbial # Main Phrase # Subject
still # isn't there # a date of mine with him

To tarate swilin b'a yet' winh t'a b'aj ay jun k'en, jun j'en nha k'e'en.
Toh táráte swílin p'ah yet' wính t'ah p'áj ʔay jun k'en, jun k'en nhá k'éʔen,"
toh tarateh tz-Ø-w-ʔil hin-p'ah y-ʔet' winh t'ah p'aj ʔay-Ø jun k'en nha-k'eʔen,"
still # date ICP-B3-A1SG-see A1SG-self A3-accompany NCLF LOC ADV exist-B3 NUM NCLF house-stone
Adverbial # Subject (appositive)
still # a date to see myself with him where there is a shelter cave,"

Chab' nok' okes chi' t'a nok' kalnel.
cháp' nok' (kón . . . nok') ʔókes chiʔ t'ah (. . . t'ah nok' . . . t'ah nok' . . .) nok' kálnél.
Ø-chih-hap' # nok' . . . ʔokes chiʔ # t'ah . . . nok' kalnel
B3-speak-REP # NCLF coyote DEM # LOC NCLF sheep
Main Phrase # Subject # Adverbial

they say spoke # the Coyote # to the Ram.

Bweno.
Bwénoh.
bwenoh
good
Intro
well

Haxob' yalan nok' ch'ak kalnel chi' t'a nok' okes chi' jun, t'a nok' koyote chi'.
Haxop' yálan nok' (nok') ch'ák kálnel chi7 t'a nok' 7ókes chi jún, t'a nok' kóyóte chi7,
ha7 xoh hap # y-7al-an # nok' ch'ak kalnel chi7 # t'ah nok' 7okes chi7 jun # t'ah nok' koyote chi7
DEM ADV REP # A3-say-DUR # NCLF sheep DEM # LOC NCLF coyote DEM CL # LOC NCLF coyote DEM
Adverbial # Main Phrase # Subject # Adverbial # Adverbial (appositive)
already then they say # said # the Ram # to the Coyote [clitic] # to that Coyote:

"Ix wil winh,
"7ix wíl wính,
7ix-Ø-w-7il # winh
CP-B3-A1SG-SEE # NCLF
Main Phrase # Object
"I saw # him

Hatik aykan'ek' winh t'a jolom lum witz chi', t'a tsalan chi'.
hátik 7áykan 7ek' wính t'a jólom lum wítz chí7, t'a tzálan chí7.
ha7 tik # 7ay-Ø-kan-7ek' # winh # t'ah jolom lum witz chi7 # t'ah tzal-an chi7
DEM DEM # exist-B3-DIR-DIR # NCLF # LOC head mountain DEM # LOC ridge DEM
Adverbial # Main Phrase # Subject # Adverbial # Adverbial
here # is over there # he # at the head of the mountain # on that ridge

Hata' ay winh, t'a yich jun te niwan taj.

Háta7 7áy wính, t'a yích jun te níwan táj.
ha7 ta7 # 7ay-Ø # winh # t'ah y-7ich jun te7 niw-an taj
DEM ADV # exist-B3 # NCLF # LOC A3-foot NUM NCLF large pine
Adverbial # Main Phrase # Subject # Adverbial
there # is # he # at the foot of a large pine tree

Hata' ayek' winh t'a b'ajay jun k'en tenam chi'.
Háta7 7áyek' wính t'a p'ájay jun k'en ténam chí7.
ha7 ta7 # 7ay-Ø-ek' # winh # t'ah p'aj 7ay-Ø jun k'en tenam chi7
DEM ADV # exist-B3-DIR # NCLF # LOC where exist-B3 NUM NCLF
    boulder DEM
Adverbial # Main Phrase # Subject # Ad verbial
there # is # he # where there is that boulder

Tanhwab'il ha k'ochi.
Tánhwap'il ha k'óchíh,"
tanh-w-ap'-il-Ø # ha-k'och-ih"
wait-DER-PTCP-DER-B3 # A2SG-arrive-ITV
Main Phrase # Object
waiting [for] # you to arrive"

Xchab' nok' kalnel chi', t'a nok' koyote chi'.
xcháp' (nok') nok' kálnel chi7, t'a nok' kóyóte chí7.
x-Ø-chi7-hap' # nok' kalnel chi7 # t'ah nok' koyote chi7
CP-B3-speak-REP # NCLF sheep DEM # LOC NCLF coyote DEM
Main Phrase # Subject # Adverbial (Indirect Object)
said, they say # that Ram # to that Coyote

Bweno.   [Closing]
Bwénoh.
bwenoh
good
Intro
well

Heh, b'at wil winh an chi'.
"Heh, p'át wíl wính 7án chí7."
heh # p'at w-7il # winh 7an # chi7

EXCLAM # DIR A1SG-see # NCLF PAR # DEM
Intro # Main Phrase # Object # Adverbial
well # I go see # him # there

B'at kan jun ch'ak kalnel chi'.
P'át kan jun ch'ák kálnel chí7.
Ø-Ø-p'at-kan jun # ch'ak kalnel chi7
CP-B3-go-DIR CL # NCLF horn sheep DEM
Main Phrase # Subject
left # that Ram

Entonse xcha'ankanb'e nok' okes.
7entónse xchá7ankan p'e nok' 7ókes.
7entonse # Ø-s-cha7-an-kan # p'eh # nok' 7okes
ADV # B3-A3SG-take-DUR-DIR # road # NCLF coyote
Intro # Main Phrase # Object # Subject
then # took # road # Coyote
                              [Second Event]
                              [Background]

B'at nok'.
P'at nók',
Ø-Ø-p'at # nok'
CP-B3-go # NCLF
Main Phrase # Subject
went # he

K'och nok' t'a b'ajtil ayek' winh konejo chi'.
k'óch nók' t'a p'ájtil 7áyek' winh kónéjo chí7.
Ø-Ø-k'och # nok' # t'ah p'aj-til 7ay-Ø-ek' winh konejo chi7
CP-B3-arrive # NCLF # LOC where-DER exist-B3-DIR NCLF rabbit DEM
Main Phrase # Subject # Adverbial
arrived # he # to where that Rabbit was

Haxob' yilan winh konejo jun.
Háxop' yílan winh (winh) kónéjo jún.
ha7 xo hap' # Ø-y-7il-an # winh konejoh # jun
DEM ADV REP # CP-A3-see-DUR # NCLF rabbit # CL
Intro # Main Phrase # Object # Clitic

then # they say he saw # the Rabbit
To k'och winh koyote.
To (k'och) k'óch winh kóyóte.
toh # Ø-Ø-k'och # winh koyote
ADV # CP-B3-arrive # NCLF coyote
Adverbial # Main Phrase # Subject
still # arrived # the Coyote

Antonse sk'anb'an yawajab' b'at, haxo winh konejo chi jun.
7antonse sk'ánp'an yáwajap' p'at, (winh) háxo winh kónéjo chi jún.
7antonse # Ø-Ø-s-k'an-p'-an # Ø-Ø-y-7aw-aj-hap' # ha7 xoh winh konejoh
    chi7 # jun
ADV # CP-B3-A3-ask-DER-DUR # CP-B3-A3-cry-DER-REP # DEM ADV NCLF
    coyote DEM # CL
Intro # Main Phrase # Main Phrase (appositive) # Object # [Clitic]
then # he asked him # he cried out to # that Rabbit there

Chek'anoch winh t'a jun icham tenam chi'.
Chék'anoch wính t'ah jun 7ícham ténam chí7.
chek'-an-Ø-och # winh # t'ah jun 7icham tenam chi7
lean-PTCP-B3-DIR # NCLF # LOC NUM large boulder DEM
Main Phrase # Subject # Adverbial
leaning was # he # on a large boulder there

To lanhan sb'at asun.
Toh lánhan sp'át 7ásun
toh lanh-an # tz-Ø-p'at # 7asun
ADV swirl-PTCP # ICP-B3-go # cloud
Adverbial # Main Phrase # Subject
still swirling # go # clouds

To lanhan sb'at asun t'a spatik k'en.
Toh lánhan sp'át 7ásun t'a spátik k'en,
toh lanh-an # tz-Ø-p'at # 7asun # t'ah s-patik k'en,
ADV swirl-PTCP # ICP-B3-go # cloud # LOC its-back stone
Adverbial # Main Phrase # Subject # Adv erbial
still swirling # go # clouds # on top of the rock

Yuj chi' to skotkan k'e'en.
yuj chí7 toh skótkan k'é7én.
y-7uj chi7 # toh # tz-Ø-kot-kan # k'e7en
A3-cause DEM # ADV # ICP-B3-draw-near-DIR # stone
Intro # Adverbial # Main Phrase # Subject
because # still # comes down # rock

Entonse ijan'och . . .
7entónse 7íjan 7och (jun jun),
7entonse # 7ij-an-Ø-och
ADV # lean-PTCP-B3-DIR
Intro # Adverbial # . . .
then # leaning against it . . .

la'an chab'il hab' sk'ab' jun konejo chi',
lá7an cháp'il hap' sk'áp' jun kónéjo chi7,
la7-an-Ø cha7-p'-il-hap' s-k'ap' jun konejo chi7,
prop-PTCP-B3 # NUM-DER-DER-REP A3-hand NUM rabbit DEM
Adverbial (Stative) # Adverbial (Instrumental),
propped [it was] # [with] two, they say, hands of the Rabbit . . .

la'an yamjinak jun k'e'en chi'.
lá7an yámjinak jun k'é7en chí7.
la7-an-Ø # yam-j-ih-nak-Ø # jun k'e7en chi7.
prop-PTCP-B3 # hold-PSV-ITV-PTCP-B3 # NUM stone DEM
Adverbial # Main Phrase # Subject
propped # was held # a rock.

Ayuch nok' yoyalok k'e'en.
7áyuch nok' yóyalok k'é7én.
7ay-Ø-uch # nok' # y-7oy-al-ok k'e7en
exist-B3-DIR # NCLF # its-support-DER-DER stone
Main Phrase # Subject # Adverbial
was # he # like a prop for the stone

Hi' to wan skotan yib'anh, sna'ani.
Hi7 toh wán skótan yíp'anh, sná7aníh.
hi7 # toh wan tz-Ø-kot-an y-7ip'-anh # tz-Ø-s-na7-an-ih

EXCLAM # ADV PROG INC-B3-draw-near-DUR A3-top-DER # ICP-B3-A3
-think-DER-ITV
Intro # Topic (Object) # Main Phrase
yes # as if it were falling over on top of him # he thought

Weno.
Wénoh.
good
Intro
well

[Dialogue]
"Tas tsa k'ulej chi'. konejo," xchab' nok' koyote chi'.
"Tás tza k'úlej chi7, kónéjoh," xcháp' nok' kóyóte chí7.
tas tz-ha-k'ul-ej chi7 konejo # Ø-s-chi7-hap' # nok' koyote chi7
Q [#] ICP-B2SG-do-TV DEM [#] rabbit # B3-A3SG-REP # NCLF coyote DEM
Topic (Object) # Main Phrase # Subject
what are you doing there, Rabbit # they say said # that Coyote

Sk'och nok' koyote t'a nok' konejo.
Sk'óch nok' kóyote t'ah nok' kónéjoh.
tz-Ø-k'och # nok' koyote # t'ah nok' konejoh
ICP-B3-arrive # NCLF coyote # LOC NCLF rabbit
Main Phrase # Subject # Adverbial (Indirect Object)
arrives # the Coyote # to the Rabbit

"Malaj.
"Málaj.
ma-Ø-laj
NEG-B3-NEG
Main Phrase
nothing

Kotanh
Kótanh
kot-anh
draw-near-IMP
Main Phrase
come here!

¡Ak' pawor!
7ák' páwor!
Ø-7ak' # pawor
IMP-do # favor
Main Phrase # Object
do # a favor

Ochanh kan t'atik.
7óchanh kan t'atik.
7och-anh-kan # t'ah tik
enter-IMP-DIR # LOC DEM
Main Phrase # Adverbial
come stay # here

¡Yam kan jun k'e'en tik!
Yám kan jun k'é7en tík!
Ø-yam-kan # jun k'e7en tik
IMP-hold-DIR # NUM stone DEM
Main Phrase # Object
stay holding # this rock

To chi' ijan skot k'e'en.
To chí7 7íjan skót k'é7én.
toh chi7 # 7ij-an # tz-Ø-kot # k'e7en
ADV DEM # lean-PTCP # ICP-B3-come-near # stone
Intro # Adverbial # Main Phrase # Subject
still # leaning # comes # stone

Pero . . . niwan hach,
Pero (tík) níwan hách,
peroh (tik) # niw-an-hach
ADV (hesitation) # big-DER-B2SG
Intro # Main Phrase
but (uh) # you are big

Ay hip.
7áy híp.
7ay-Ø # h-7ip

exist-B3 # A2SG-strength
Main Phrase # Subject
there is # your strength

Ichamom ha te'el.
7íchamom ha té7él.
7icham-om-Ø # ha-te7-al
great-DER-B3 # A2SG-tall-DER
Main Phrase # Subject
big is # your height

A, ol hak' yet'ok.
7á, 7ol hák' yét'ok.
7ah # 7ol-Ø-h-7ak' # y-et'-ok
EXCLAM # FUT-B3-A2SG-do # A3-with-DER
Intro # Main Phrase # Adverbial
oh # you will do it # with it

¡Tik yam kani!
Tík yám kaníh!
tik # Ø-yam-kan-ih
DEM # IMP-hold-DIR-ITV
Adverbial # Main Phrase
here # stay holding on

B'atin say chab'ok koy.
P'atin sáy (sáy) cháp'ok kóy.
p'at Ø-hin-say # chap'-ok k-7oy
go B3-A1SG-search # NUM-DER A1SG-support
Main Phrase # Object
go I to find # a couple of my props

To ka te oy kak'kanoch t'atik,
To ká te 7óy kák'kanoch t'atik,
toh kah # te7 7oy # Ø-k-7ak'-an-och # t'ah tik...
ADV ADV # NCLF support # B3-A1PL-give-DUR-DIR # LOC DEM
Intro # Topic (Object) # Main Phrase # Adverbial # ...
still # wooden prop # we put it in # here

Yik manh ol lanhchaj jun k'e'en tik,"
yík manh 7ol lánhchaj jun k'é7en tík,"
y-7ik ma-nh 7ol-Ø-lanh-ch-aj jun k'e7en tik
A3-reason # NEG-NEG FUT-B3-felled-PSV-DER NUM stone DEM
Adverbial # Main Phrase # Subject
so that it will not fall over, this stone

xchab' nok' konejo chi' t'a nok' koyote chi'.
xcháp' nok' kónéjo chí7 t'a nok' kóyóte chí7.
Ø-s-chi7-hap' # nok' konejoh chi7 # t'ah nok' koyte chi7
B3-A3-say-REP # NCLF rabbit DEM # LOC NCLF coyote DEM
Main Phrase # Subject # Indirect Object
said, they say # that Rabbit # to that Coyote

"Sta wyen," xchab' nok' koyote chi'.
"Stá wyén," xcháp' nok' kóyóte chí7.
"está bién" # Ø-Ø-s-chi7-hap' # nok' koyote chi7
"está bién" # CP-B3-A3-say-REP # NCLF coyote DEM
Topic (Object) # Main Phrase # Subject
"OK" # said, they say # the Coyote

[Closing]

Yochkan
Yóch kan
Ø-y-7och-kan
B3-A3-want-DIR
Main Phrase
he wanted to stay

ijan nok' koyote chi'.
7íjan nok' kóyóte chí7.
7ij-an-Ø # nok' koyote chi7
lean-PTCP-DER-B3 # coyote DEM
Main Phrase # Subject
leaning # that Coyote

Hi, yochkan wets'wets' t'a jun tenam chi'.
Hí, yóch kan wétz'wetz' t'a jun ténam chí7.
hi7 # Ø-y-7och-kan # wetz'-wetz' # t'a jun tenam chi7

EXCLAM # B3-A3-want-DIR # pushing # LOC NUM boulder DEM
Intro # Main Phrase # Adverbial # Adverbial
yes # he wanted to stay # pushing # on that boulder

Lanhan sb'ey asun.
Lánhan sp'éy 7ásún.
lanh-an # tz-Ø-p'ey # 7asun
swirl-PTCP-DER # ICP-B3-go # cloud
Adverbial # Main Phrase # Subject
swirling # goes # cloud

[Third (Peak) Event]
[Background]

Ke, te k'itax chi', ayxom junok ora sb'at nok' konejo chi',
Ké, te k'ítax chí7, 7áyxom júnok 7óra sp'át nok' (nok') kónéjo chí7,
ke # teh k'it-ax chi7 # 7ay-Ø-xoh-ham # jun-ok 7orah tz-Ø-p'at nok' kone-
joh chi7...
EXCLAM # ADV while DEM # exist-B3-ADV-DUB # NUM-IRR hour ICP-
B3-GO NCLF rabbit DEM
Intro # Adverbial # Main Phrase # Subject...
so # much later # it was about # an hour [since] the Rabbit left...

tek'tek' wal aj winh koyote chi'.
(ték'p'anh) ték'tek' wal 7áj winh (winh) kóyóte chí7.
tek'-tek' # wal Ø-7aj # winh koyote chi7
straight up # PROG B3-stand # NCLF coyote DEM
Adverbial # Main Phrase Subject
straight up # was standing up # that Coyote

Yel nhilnaj winh t'a yalanh k'en tenam,
Yél nhílnaj wính t'ah yálanh k'en ténam,
Ø-y-7el # nhil-n-aj # winh # t'ah y-7al-anh k'en tenam
B3-A3-left # leaping # NCLF # LOC A3-base-DER NCLF boulder
Main Phrase # Adverbial # Subject # Adverbial [unusual syntax]
left it # leaping # he # at the foot of the boulder

Sna'ani yemkan naynaj jun tenam chi',
sná7anih yém kan náynaj jun ténam chí7,
Ø-s-na7-an-ih # Ø-y-7em-kan nay-n-aj jun tenam chi7

B3-A3-think-DUR-ITV # B3-A3-drop-DIR slowly NUM boulder DEM
Main Phrase # Object
he was thinking # the boulder was slowly falling over

sna'an winh koyote chi'.
sná7an winh (winh) kóyóte chí7.
Ø-s-na7-an # winh koyote chi7
B3-A3-think-DUR # NCLF coyote DEM
Main Phrase # Subject
was thinking # the Coyote

Tikni malaj k'en tenam chi' telwi.
Tik ni málaj k'en ténam chí7 télwíh.
tik nih # ma-Ø-laj # k'en tenam chi7 Ø-tel-w-ih
DEM ADV # NEG-B3-NEG # NCLF boulder DEM B3-fall-DER-ITV
Intro # Main Phrase # Subject [Unusual syntax <*ma-telwih-laj k'en
    tenam chi7]
but # it wasn't # that boulder falling

Hanheja' yaj k'e'en.
Hánhejá7 yáj k'é7én.
ha7-nhej-ha7 # y-7aj # k'e7en
DEM-ADV-DEM # A3-stay # stone
Adverbial # Main Phrase # Subject
just like that # was # the stone (it just stayed there)

Hi', malaj ik'an k'en.
Hí7, # málaj 7ík'an k'én.
hi7, # ma-Ø-laj 7ik'-an # k'en
EXCLAM # NEG-B3-NEG happen # stone
Intro # Main Phrase # Subject
Yes # nothing happened # [to] stone

Wénoh.
wenoh
good
Intro
well

[Dialogue (Peak)]

"Tob'an tonhej tsin yak' joder winh.   [Couplet Part A]
"Tóp'an tónhej tzin yák' jóder winh.
top'-an # toh-nhej # tz-hin y-7ak' joder # winh
perhaps # just # ICP-B1SG-A3-do screw # NCLF
Intro # Adverbial # Main Phrase # Subject
maybe # just # is screwing me # he

Tob'an tonhej tsin yak' joder winh konejo tik.   [Couplet Part B]
Tóp'an tónhej tzin yák' jóder winh kónéjo tík.
top'-an # toh-nhej # tz-hin y-7ak' joder # winh konejoh tik
perhaps # just # ICP-B1SG-A3-do screw # NCLF rabbit DEM
Intro # Adverbial # Main Phrase # Subject
maybe # just # is screwing me # this Rabbit

Tak olin lajeli.   [Triplet Part A]
Ták 7olin lájelih.
tak # 7ol-Ø-hin-laj-el-ih
perhaps # FUT-B3-A1SG-finish-DIR-ITV
Intro # Main Phrase
perhaps # I will finish him

Tak tekan to, olin mila',   [Triplet Part B]
Ták tékan tóh, (7ol) 7olin mílá7,
tak # tek-an toh # 7ol-Ø-hin-mil-ha7
perhaps # still # FUT-B3-A1SG-kill-TV
Intro # Adverbial # Main Phrase
perhaps # still # I will kill him

to olin say hin k'olok,"   [Triplet Part C]
tóh 7olin sáy hin k'ólok,"
toh # 7ol-Ø-hin-say # hin-k'olok,
still # FUT-B3-A1SG-search # A1SG-enemy
Adverbial # Main Phrase # Object
still # I will look for # my enemy

xchab' winh koyote chi'.
xcháp' winh kóyóte chi7.

Ø-s-chi7-hap' # winh koyote chi7
B3-A3-say-REP # NCLF coyote DEM
Main Phrase # Subject
said, they say # that Coyote

B'atchi winh.   [Closing]
P'átchih wính.
Ø-Ø-p'at-x-ih # winh
CP-B3-go-REPET-ITV # NCLF
Main Phrase # Subject
went again # he

[The scene changes, and another set of episodes in the series begins immediately.]

Academia de Lenguas Mayas de Guatemala. 2003. *Spaxti'al Slolonelal; Vocabulario Chuj. Chuj-Kaxlanh ti', Kaxlanh ti'-Chuj.* Guatemala: Academia de Lenguas Mayas de Guatemala.

Aissen, Judith, Nora C. England, and Roberto Zavala Maldonado, eds. 2017. *The Mayan Languages.* London: Routledge.

Andrade, Manuel J. 1946. Materials on the Mam, Jacalteca, Aguacatec, Chuj, Bachajon, Palencano, and Lacandon Languages. Microfilm Collection of Manuscripts on Middle American Cultural Anthropology, No. 10.

Bassie-Sweet, Karen. 2008. *Maya Sacred Geography and the Creator Deities.* Norman: University of Oklahoma Press.

Berlin, O. Brent, Nicholas A. Hopkins, and Norman A. McQuown. 1969. *Huehuetenango vocabularies, 1961, 1962.* Collected on magnetic tape and transcribed by O. Brent Berlin, Nicholas A. Hopkins and Norman A. McQuown. Microfilm Collection of Manuscripts on Middle American Cultural Anthropology. Joseph Regenstein Library, University of Chicago.

Blom, Frans, and Oliver LaFarge. 1926–27. *Tribes and Temples.* 2 vols. Middle American Research Institute, Publication 1. New Orleans: Tulane University.

Breedlove, Dennis, and Nicholas A. Hopkins. 1970–71. A study of Chuj (Mayan) plants, with notes on their uses, I–III. *The Wasmann Journal of Biology* 28(2): 275–98, 1970; 29(1): 107–28, 1971; 29(2): 189–205, 1971.

Bright, William. 1967. Inventory of descriptive materials. In *Handbook of Middle American Indians,* vol. 5: *Linguistics,* ed. Norman A. McQuown, pp. 9–62. Austin: University of Texas Press.

Buenrostro Diaz, Elsa Cristina. 2002. La voz antipasiva y el enfoque de agente en el chuj de San Mateo Ixtatán. *Anales de Antropología* 36:229–47.

———. 2004. El sufijo *-an* en el chuj de San Mateo Ixtatán. *Anales de Antropología* 38:255–67.

———. 2005. La voz en chuj y tojolabal. *Anales de Antropología* 39(1):219–30.

———. 2007. Oraciones de complemento en chuj de San Mateo Ixtatán. *Anales de Antropología* 41(1):239–66.

———. 2013. La voz en chuj de San Mateo Ixtatán. Ph.D. dissertation, El Colegio de México.

Campbell, Lyle. 2017. Mayan history and comparison. In *The Mayan Languages,* eds. Judith Aissen, Nora C. England, and Roberto Zavala Maldonado, pp. 43–61. London: Routledge.

Carmack, Robert M, ed. 1988. *Harvest of Violence: The Maya Indians and the Guatemalan Crisis*. Norman: University of Oklahoma Press.

Christenson, Allen J. 2007. *Popol Vuh: The Sacred Book of the Maya*. Norman: University of Oklahoma Press.

Colby, Benjamin N., and Lore M. Colby. 1981. *The Daykeeper: The Life and Discourse of an Ixil Diviner*. Cambridge: Harvard University Press.

Conklin, Harold C. 1962. Lexicographic treatment of folk taxonomies. In *Problems in Lexicography*, eds. Fred W. Householder and Sol Saporta, pp. 119–41. Indiana University Research Center in Anthropology, Folklore, and Linguistics, Publication 21.

Coon, Jessica. 2016. Unergatives, antipassives, and roots in Chuj. In *Proceedings of CILLA: The Conference on Indigenous Languages in Latin America*. AILLA (Archive of the Indigenous Languages of Latin America), University of Texas at Austin.

Coon, Jessica, and Elizabeth Carolan. 2017. Nominalizations and the structure of progressives in Chuj Mayan. *Glossa: A Journal of General Linguistics* 2(1):22. 1–35, DOI: https://doi.org/10.5334/gjgl.51.

Diarassouba, Sidiky. 2007. Establishment of literary standards for an oral language: the case of Nafara oral discourse patterns, Côte d'Ivoire, West Africa. Ph.D. dissertation, Florida State University.

Dirección General de Cartografía. 1962. *Diccionario Geografico de Guatemala*. 2 vols. Guatemala, CA: Dirección General de Cartografía.

Dirección General de Estadística. 1950. *Sexto Censo de Población, República de Guatemala*. Guatemala, CA: Dirección General de Estadística.

Ekstrom, David. 1961. *A Sbabel Carta San Pablo Da Eb Aj Corinto*. Guatemala: Sociedad Bíblica Americana.

Falla, Ricardo. 1983. *Voices of the Survivors: The Massacre at Finca San Francisco, Guatemala*. Cambridge, MA: Cultural Survival and Anthropology Resource Center.

Felipe Diego, Mateo, and Juan Gaspar Juan. 1998. *Diccionario del idioma Chuj*. Antigua, Guatemala: Proyecto Lingüístico Francisco Marroquín.

Furbee, Louanna, ed. 1980. *Mayan Texts III*. IJAL-NATS (International Journal of American Linguistics, Native American Texts Series) Monograph No. 5. Chicago: University of Chicago Press. [On-line publication with a new Preface, 2015, available through the Press].

Grinevald Craig, Colette. 1978. The Rabbit and the Coyote (Jacaltec). In *Coyote Stories*, ed. William Bright. IJAL-NATS (*International Journal of American Linguistics*, Native American Texts Series), Monograph No. 1. Chicago: University of Chicago Press. pp. 184–93.

———. 1990. Clasificadores nominales: una innovación Q'anjob'al. in *Lecturas sobre la lingüística maya*, eds. Nora C. England and Stephen R. Elliott, pp. 253–68. La Antigua Guatemala: CIRMA (Centro de Investigaciones Regionales de Mesoamérica) and Plumsock Mesoamerican Studies.

Guiteras Holmes, Calixta. 1951. El calpulli de San Pablo Chalchihuitan. In Antonio Pompa y Pompa, Ignacio Marquina, and Eusabio Dávalos, eds., *Homenaje al Doctor Alfonso Caso*, pp. 190–206. México, DF: Imprenta Nuevo Mundo.

———. 1961. *Perils of the Soul: The World View of a Tzotzil Indian*. New York: The Free Press of Glencoe.

Hopkins, Nicholas A. 1964a. A Phonology of Zinacantán Tzotzil. M.A. thesis, University of Chicago.

———. 1964b. Sociocultural aspects of linguistic distributions (a preliminary study of Tzeltal and Tzotzil dialects). Microfilm Collection of Manuscripts on American Cultural Anthropology. Series X, No. 62. Chicago: University of Chicago Library.

———. 1967a. The Chuj Language. Ph.D. dissertation, University of Chicago.

———. 1967b. A Short Sketch of Chalchihuitán Tzotzil. *Anthropological Linguistics* 9(4): 9–25.

———. 1969. A Formal Account of Chalchihuitán Tzotzil Kinship Terminology. *Ethnology* 8(1):85–102.

———. 1970a. Estudio preliminar de los dialectos del tzeltal y del tzotzil. In Norman A. McQuown and Julian Pitt-Rivers, eds., *Ensayos de Antropología en la Zona Central de Chiapas*, pp. 185–214. Colección de Antropología Social, 8. México, DF: Instituto Nacional Indigenista.

———. 1970b. Numeral classifiers in Tzeltal, Jacaltec, and Chuj (Mayan). In *Papers from the Sixth Regional Meeting of the Chicago Linguistic Society, April 16–18, 1970*; pp. 23–35. Chicago: Chicago Linguistic Society.

———. 1972. Compound place names in Chuj and other Mayan languages. In Munro S. Edmonson, ed., *Meaning in Mayan Languages: Ethnolinguistic Studies*, pp. 165–82. The Hague: Mouton.

———. 1974. Historical and sociocultural aspects of the distribution of linguistic variants in Highland Chiapas, Mexico. In Ben Blount and Mary Sanches, eds., *Sociocultural Dimensions of Language Change*, pp. 185–225. New York: Academic Press.

———. 1980a. Chuj animal names and their classification. *Journal of Mayan Linguistics* 2(1):13–39.

———. 1980b. A San Mateo Chuj text. In Louanna Furbee, ed., *Mayan Texts III,* pp. 89–106. IJAL-NATS (*International Journal of American Linguistics*, Native American Texts Series) Monograph No. 5. Chicago: University of Chicago Press.

———. 1988. Classic Maya kinship systems: epigraphic and ethnographic evidence for patrilineality. *Estudios de Cultura Maya* 17:87–121.

———. 1991. Classic and modern relationship terms and the 'child of mother' glyph (T I:606.23). In Merle Greene Robertson, ed., *Sixth Palenque Round Table, 1986*, pp. 255–65. Norman: University of Oklahoma Press.

———. 2006. The place of maize in indigenous Mesoamerican folk taxonomies. In John E. Staller, Robert H. Tykot, and Bruce F. Benz, eds., *Histories of Maize:*

Multidisciplinary Approaches to the Prehistory, Biogeography, Domestication, and Evolution of Maize, Part II: *Mesoamerica, Central and South America*, pp. 611–22. San Diego: Elsevier/Academic Press.

———. 2012a. *A Dictionary of the Chuj (Mayan) Language as Spoken in San Mateo Ixtatán, Huehuetenango, Guatemala, ca. 1964–65.* Online publication: www.famsi. org/mayawriting/dictionary/hopkins/dictionaryChuj.html.

———. 2012b. The noun classifiers of Cuchumatán Mayan languages: a case of diffusion from Otomanguean. *International Journal of American Linguistics* 78(3):411–27. [A corrected table 2 was published in IJAL 78(4):595.]

Hopkins, Nicholas A., and J. Kathryn Josserand, eds. 1979. *Estudios lingüísticos en lenguas otomangues.* Colección Científica, 68. México, DF: Instituto Nacional de Antropología e Historia.

———. 1994. Pasado, presente y futuro en la lingüística maya. In *Panorama de los estudios de las lenguas indígenas de México*, eds. Leonardo Manrique, Yolanda Lastra and Doris Bartholomew, Tomo I, pp. 269–333. Colección Biblioteca Abya-Yala, 16. Quito, Ecuador: Ediciones Abya-Yala.

———. 2016. *Chol (Mayan) Folktales; a Collection of Stories from the Modern Maya of Southern Mexico.* Boulder: University Press of Colorado.

Hull, Kerry M., and Michael D. Carrasco, eds. 2012. *Parallel Worlds: Genre, Discourse, and Poetics in Contemporary, Colonial, and Classic Maya Literature.* Boulder: University Press of Colorado.

Hymes, Dell. 1964. *Language in Culture and Society: A Reader in Linguistics and Anthropology.* New York: Harper & Row.

Josserand, J. Kathryn. 1975. Archaeological and linguistic correlations for Mayan prehistory. *Actas del XLI Congreso Internacional de Americanistas, México, 2 al 7 de septiembre de 1974*, pp. 501–10. México: Instituto Nacional de Antropología.

———. 1991. The narrative structure of hieroglyphic texts at Palenque. In *Sixth Palenque Round Table, 1986*, ed. Merle Greene Robertson, 12–31. Norman: University of Oklahoma Press.

———. 2016. The narrative structure of Chol folktales. In *Chol (Mayan) Folktales*, Nicholas A. Hopkins and J. Kathryn Josserand, pp. 15–31. Boulder: University Press of Colorado.

Josserand, J. Kathryn, and Nicholas A. Hopkins. 2011. Directions and Partitions in Maya World View. On-line publication: www.famsi.org/research/hopkins/directions.html.

Josserand, J. Kathryn, with Nicholas A. Hopkins, Ausencio Cruz Guzmán, Ashley Kistler, and Kayla Price. 2003. *Story Cycles in Chol (Mayan) Mythology: Contextualizing Classic Iconography.* Report of a Project Sponsored by the Foundation for the Advancement of Mesoamerican Studies, Inc. (FAMSI), Crystal River, Florida; FAMSI grant number 01085.

Kaufman, Terrence S. 1978. Meso-American Languages. *Encyclopedia Britannica*, 15th Edition, vol. 11: 956–63.

———. 2017. Aspects of the lexicon of proto-Mayan and its earliest descendants. In *The Mayan Languages*, eds. Judith Aissen, Nora C. England, and Roberto Zavala Maldonado, pp. 62–111. London: Routledge.

Kaufman, Terrence S., with John Justeson. 2003. A Preliminary Mayan Etymological Dictionary. www.albany.edu/pdlma, and www.famsi.org/dictionaries.

Krueger, Chris, ed. 1982. *Guatemala: Government against the People*. Washington, DC: Washington Office on Latin America.

LaFarge, Oliver. 1947. *Santa Eulalia: The Religion of a Cuchumatan Indian Town*. Chicago: University of Chicago Press.

LaFarge, Oliver, and Douglas Byers. 1931. *The Year Bearer's People*. Middle American Research Institute, Publication 3. New Orleans: Tulane University.

Lenguas Mayas de Guatemala. 1988. *Documento de referencia para la pronunciación de los nuevos alfabetos oficiales*. Guatemala: Instituto Indigenista Nacional, Ministerio de Cultura y Deportes.

Longacre, Robert E. 1985. Discourse peak as zone of turbulence. In *Beyond the Sentence: Discourse and Sentential Form*, ed. Jessica R. Wirth, pp. 81–98. Ann Arbor, MI: Karoma.

Manz, Beatriz. 1988. *Refugees of a Hidden War: The Aftermath of Counterinsurgency in Guatemala*. Albany: State University of New York Press.

Mateo Toledo, Eladio. 2017. Q'anjob'al. In *The Mayan Languages*, eds. Judith Aissen, Nora C. England, and Roberto Zavala Maldonado, pp. 533–69. London: Routledge.

Maurer, David. 1940. *The Big Con*. Indianapolis: Bobbs-Merrill.

Maxwell, Judith. 1976. Chuj intransitives: or when can an intransitive verb take an object? M*ayan Linguistics* 1:128–40.

———. 1978a. Chuj clause collapsing. In *Papers in Mayan Linguistics* (Studies in Mayan Linguistics, No. 2), ed. Nora England, pp. 127–35. University of Missouri, Miscellaneous Publications in Anthropology, No. 6.

———. 1978b. How to talk to people who talk *chekel* "different": the Chuj (Mayan) solution. Ph.D. dissertation, University of Chicago.

———. 1981. For you a special language—Market Chuj. *Papers from the Parasession on Language and Behavior of the Seventeenth Regional Meeting of the Chicago Linguistic Society*, pp. 149–55. Chicago: Chicago Linguistic Society.

———. 1989. Some aspects of Chuj discourse. *Anthropological Linguistics* 29:4.

———. 1990. El discurso en Chuj. In *Lecturas en la Lingüística Maya*, ed. Nora England and Stephen Elliott, pp. 445–59. Lecturas Sobre la Lingüística Maya, Guatemala, CA: Centro de Investigaciones Regionales de Mesoamérica, La Antigua Guatemala and Plumsock Mesoamerican Studies, South Woodstock, VT.

———. 1996. Chuj (Maya). In *Encyclopedia of World Cultures*, vol. 8: *Middle America and the Caribbean*, ed. James Dow, pp. 70–74. Boston: G. K. Hall & Co.

———. 2001. *Textos chujes de San Mateo Ixtatán*. Palos Verdes, CA: Fundación Yax Te'.

Mayers, Marvin, ed. 1966. *Languages of Guatemala*. Janua Linguarum, Series Practica, no. 23. The Hague: Mouton.

McQuown, Norman A. 1967. History of studies in Middle American Linguistics. In Norman A. McQuown, ed., *Handbook of Middle American Indians*, vol. 5, *Linguistics*, pp. 3–7. Austin: University of Texas Press.

McQuown, Norman A., and Julian Pitt-Rivers, eds. 1970. *Ensayos de Antropología en la Zona Central de Chiapas*. Colección de Antropología Social, 8. México, DF: Instituto Nacional Indigenista.

Mondloch, James L. 1980. K'e'x: Quiché naming. *Journal of Mayan Languages* 1(2):9–25.

Morris, Walter F. ("Chip"), Jr. 2010. *Guía textil de los Altos de Chiapas*. San Cristóbal de Las Casas: Asociación Cultural Na Bolom.

Oakes, Maud. 1951. *The Two Crosses of Todos Santos; Survivals of Mayan Religious Festivals*. Bollingen Series XXVII. New York: Pantheon Books.

PAVA (Programa de Ayuda para los Vecinos del Altiplano). 1984. *Final Report*. Washington. DC: USAID Project No. DR-520-84-04.

Pitarch Ramón, Pedro. 1996. *Ch'ulel: una etnografía de las almas tzeltales*. Mexico, DF: Fondo de Cultura Económica.

Recinos, Adrián. 1954. *Monografía del Departamento de Huehuetenango*. Second edition. Guatemala: Editorial del Ministro de Educación Pública.

Strehlow, T. G. H. 1947. *Aranda Traditions*. Melbourne: Melbourne University Press.

Swadesh, Mauricio [Morris]. 1961. Interrelaciones de las lenguas mayas. *Anales del Instituto Nacional de Antropología e Historia* 42:231–67.

Vásquez Álvarez, Juan Jesús. 2001. *Palabras floridas; pejkaj ch'utyaty. Actividad oral de los choles dedicada a las deidades*. Tuxtla Gutiérrez: Gobierno del Estado de Chiapas.

Vogt, Evon Z. 1994. *Fieldwork among the Maya: Reflections on the Harvard Chiapas Project*. Albuquerque: University of New Mexico Press.

Wagley, Charles. 1969. The Maya of Northwestern Guatemala. In *Handbook of Middle American Indians*, vol. 7: *Ethnology, Part One*, Evon Z. Vogt, ed., pp. 46–68. Austin: University of Texas Press.

Williams, Kenneth. 1963a. *A Yaxbil Dios Tz'ibbil can yuj San Pablo*. Guatemala: Sociedad Bíblica en Guatemala.

———. 1963b. *A Wach' Abx 'ix Tz'ibj can San Marcos*. Guatemala: Sociedad Bíblica en Guatemala.

———. 1963c. *A Tas 'ix Bo eb Schech Jesús*. Guatemala: Sociedad Bíblica en Guatemala.

Williams, Kenneth, and Barbara Williams. 1966. Chuj. In *Languages of Guatemala*, ed. Marvin K. Mayers, pp. 219–34. Janua Linguarum, Series Practica, No. 23. The Hague: Mouton.

INDEX

Page numbers in italics indicate illustrations.

Academia de Lenguas Mayas de
Guatemala, 10, 20, 43, 126
Amatenango, Chiapas, 4
Andrade, Manuel J., 7
Androcles and the Lion, 52
animal classes, 32, 53
Archive of the Indigenous Languages of
Latin America (AILLA), 9, 15, 20, 22,
24, 42, 126, 144
Avant, John, 8

Barillas, *4*, 41, 101, 110
Berlin, O. Brent, 13–14, 16
Breedlove, Dennis, 15, *16*, 52
Br'er Rabbit, 22, 31
Bu'ul (*B'u'ul*), 104
Buenrostro, Cristina, 24, 42
Bulej (*B'ulej*), *6*, 108

Canán, Cananá (*Kanan*), 97, 101, 109
Canquintic (*K'ankintik*), *18*
card games, 43, 48
cardinal directions, 112
Centro de Investigaciones Superiores en
Antropología Social (CIESAS), 16
Centro de Investigaciones
Superiores del Instituto Nacional
de Antropología e Historia
(CIS-INAH), 16
Chiapanec, 13, 130
Chiapas Study Projects, 7, 13
civil war (*la violencia*), 9–10, 23, 96–109
climate, 3–4, *19*

clothing: men's jacket or capixay (*lopil*),
3–4, *6*, 25, 66; women's dress or huipil
(*nip*), 5, *18*, *25*
Comitán, Chiapas, 4, 11
composition of humans, 53, 64–66
Coon, Jessica, 10, 42
couplets: lexical couplets, 28, 32, 33, 36,
145; syntactic couplets, 36
Cuchumatán Mountains, 12–13, *14*,
52, 65, 130
cultural innovation, 25–26

Day, Christopher, 16
diviners, 43, 45–46
Documenting Endangered Languages
Fellowship (National Endowment for
the Humanities), 18, 20

Earth Lord, 54
editing texts, 24–25
Ekstrom, David, 7
El Aguacate (*Onh*), 96–109
El Quetzal (*Ketsal*), 96–98, 100, 108
Elias, Paulina, 42
Erythrina species (*chum*), 43
ethnography, 19

Finca San Francisco (*Samran*), 97–98,
102, 105, 107
Florida State University, 18
Foundation for the Advancement
of Mesoamerican Studies, Inc.
(FAMSI), 20